"This book that you hold in your hands will transform your life, your relationships, and the life of your LGBTQ+ teen.

"Heather is a loving and masterful guide. When you read and, more importantly, implement what you learn in this book, you will deepen your understanding and learn how to navigate the transition with your family member. As you dive into the pages, you will sense her genuine, kind, and calm presence leading you through her four pillars of Embrace, Educate (and Unlearn Bias), Empower, and Love. Heather is the real deal, and she has condensed the lessons that she and her family have mastered through their own transition.

"Believe me, she fully understands your doubts and fears, the difficulties and the pain, and she can help you find the joy and love you desire too. Spend time with her to *ponder and reflect*, and make this path your own.

"If you want a more loving relationship with your coming out teen and you want to be an ally and advocate in an honest wholehearted way, then I would encourage you to buy this book. Use it and share the lessons widely so that we can make this a more inclusive, encouraging, and accepting world."

Candy Motzek, BASc, CPCC, PCC Business+Soul coach

"Heather Hester has written a beautiful and poignant must-read for any parent or caregiver raising an LGBTQ+ identified youth, no matter where they or you are on your journey. Infused with first-hand wisdom and transparency, Heather has the ability to tackle tough and realistic issues facing the LGBTQ+ community and their families in such a warm and inviting way. Through the use of humor and heartfelt personal experiences, she opens up to you about grief, despair, fear, celebration, and love, as if you were sitting and having a warm cup of coffee together. I wish this book existed when I was coming out, so my mom wouldn't have felt so alone and could have taken comfort in knowing there were other parents out there going through similar journeys."

Kate Versage, LGBTQ+ life coach and expressive arts therapist

"If you're the parent of a queer child, Heather Hester has written THE book you need to have on your nightstand. Coming from a place of such deep and profound understanding, straight from her own heart and lived experience, Heather generously gifts us all of her first-hand knowledge and understanding about raising a queer child so that we can all benefit from her life lessons and truly learn to parent our children with pride and love. If you want to be more than just an ally to your child, *Parenting with Pride* will lovingly guide you to becoming their greatest champion and partner as they navigate the complex world around them. By virtue of her honesty and candidness, you'll feel like you have an instant friend who understands the nuances of the emotions, challenges, and issues facing families raising LGBTQ+ children. A must-read for anyone raising and loving a queer child."

Lisa Sugarman, author, columnist,
Trevor Project crisis counselor, and mental health advocate

"In *Parenting with Pride*, Heather Hester shares the story of her son coming out as gay and her family's journey of acceptance and understanding with honesty, wisdom, and love. With personal anecdotes, best-practice tips for support, and sections for the reader to ponder and reflect on their own journey, Heather's book is a must-read for anyone raising an LGBTQ+ child or teen. *Parenting with Pride* feels like a warm hug from a protective mama bear."

Jeannie Gainsburg, author of *The Savvy Ally:*
A Guide for Becoming a Skilled LGBTQ+ Advocate

"*Parenting with Pride* is a timely and relevant book for families today. Not only is it informative, but Heather has made one of the most important contributions we can make—she's taken valuable lessons from her own life and used them for the sake of good on behalf of others. *Parenting with Pride* is a book that will change lives."

Chris Tompkins, author of *Raising LGBTQ Allies: A Parent's Guide*
to Changing the Messages from the Playground

"Finally there is a book I can recommend to my listeners that is honest, empowering, full of love and acceptance and setting the tone for a peaceful & joyful family life while giving parents accessible information, support, mental shifts and hope in being catalysts for change in their own communities. Thank you to Heather, Connor, and your whole family for sharing your light with this world."

Michelle Abraham, #13 Top 50 Moms in Podcasting from *Podcast*
Magazine* and host of *Blissful Parenting Podcast

"Heather Hester's new book *Parenting with Pride* is a wonderful guide for parents of LGBTQ+ children. The author draws on her family experience of supporting her gay son and her experience as a coach, advocate, and podcaster. She provides valuable practical advice on navigating challenges, unlearning biases, and learning how to best support and advocate for an LGBTQ+ child. You will find practical exercises, including journaling, self-care, and information about additional resources. The book is full of love, the main force empowering parents on this journey."

Andrew Zanevsky, President of PFLAG Council of Northern Illinois

Parenting with Pride

Unlearn Bias and Embrace, Empower, and Love Your LGBTQ+ Teen

HEATHER HESTER

Published by Familius LLC, www.familius.com
PO Box 1249, Reedley, CA 93654

Familius books are available at special discounts for bulk purchases, whether for sales promotions or for family or corporate use. For more information, contact Familius Sales at orders@familius.com.

Special thanks to AnneMoss Rodgers and Mental Health Awareness Education for granting persmission to use the Metal Health Coping Card, created based on research by doctors Craig Brian and David Rudd.

Library of Congress Control Number: 2024932047

Print ISBN 9781641709125
Ebook ISBN 9781641704410

Printed in the United States of America

Edited by Michele Robbins and Peg Sandkam
Sensitivity Reader: Kenneth Creech
Cover design by Carlos Mireles-Guerrero
Book design by Brooke Jorden

10 9 8 7 6 5 4 3 2 1

First Edition

Contents

For Connor, whose courage and extraordinary spirit ignited this beautiful, life-changing journey for all of us. My love and gratitude for you are endless.

*T*wo thousand miles from home, I received a call that my sixteen-year-old son was missing. A search that lasted into the early hours of the morning culminated with a call and a single sentence: "Mom, I'm gay." My response? "Thank God! I thought you were dead!" Through our tears of relief, my darling boy started to explain what brought him to this terrifying point, and thus, our journey began.

More than six years have now passed, and we've experienced growth that has been anything but linear. I say *we* because when your child comes out as LGBTQ+, it involves shifts, growth, and learning for the entire family—not just the one who's connecting with their sexual orientation and/or gender identity.

The learning curve for the first year and a half was more like a steep, jagged incline than a gentle curve. As my son—the oldest of four, the overachiever and rule-follower—took a 180-degree turn in every possible way, we encountered substance use and abuse, extreme self-loathing, mental health issues (including extreme anxiety and deep depression), dangerous behaviors, and a suicide attempt all in just the first few months. And this was with unconditional love and complete support from his immediate family.

My husband and I scrambled to learn and to find resources and support. We were pitifully unprepared and frustrated as we could not find the support options we needed or research and resources readily available past national organizations such as PFLAG (formerly Parents, Families, and Friends of Lesbians and Gays) and The Trevor Project.

When we hit the eye of the storm in late 2018, I set out to create what we could not find. I couldn't bear the thought of other families going through what we did: the fear for your child's safety, the sleepless nights, the endless worry, the frustration, the heartbreak of just wanting to help and support your child and not being able to find help anywhere!

I wanted other parents to know that they were not alone and that there was nothing wrong with them or their family. I wanted parents to know that their child embracing that they are gay or lesbian or transgender or any other sexual orientation and/or gender identity was not a choice, but who they inherently are. So, I set out to build a safe space where others could find the help and support we wish we'd had throughout our storm.

In the summer of 2018, I created a blog and resource-filled website called Chrysalis Mama so that I had a place to list and add incredible research, books, websites, and other resources as I found them. In November 2019, I launched my podcast, *Just Breathe: Parenting Your LGBTQ Teen*, knowing so many families desperately need this information but are either too overwhelmed or too frightened to reach out. I still host solo and interview episodes, and it sits in the top 2 percent of all podcasts worldwide. Since February 2021, I've launched my digital course, Learning to Just Breathe, one-on-one coaching for parents, speaking engagements for organizations, and an e-book and workshop called *The Language of LGBTQIA+*.

There are so many lessons we've learned. Crises, internal shifts, and evolution do not occur in a vacuum. What Steve, Connor, Isabelle, Grace, Rowan, and I experienced affected each of us deeply. Each of us has had our own challenges and shifts within our greater family dynamic. I am deeply grateful for the guidance, both spiritual and otherwise, that has supported and helped us as individuals and as a family, and I am in awe of the beautiful spirit and resilience of each of my kids and my husband. This book is my love letter of sorts to every person out there who sees themselves in our story. You are not alone.

Out of the greatest despairs come the greatest gifts.

—UNKNOWN

As if caught in an endless nightmare, I flail. Darkness is all around me. In the distance, I see an inviting light, a warmth that draws me, but I can't quite get there. I am frozen. Fear grips my chest. Terror and uncertainty cloud my mind, making every decision and every thought feel like it is life or death. But the light beckons. It finds strength I knew not was there.

I wrote this in my journal soon after Connor came out as gay. This is where I lived for a while. In the space between leaving the comfort of all I thought I knew and entering a new world of mind-expanding, life-altering awesomeness.

Does that feel familiar to you?

Has your child recently come out to you as lesbian, gay, bisexual, transgender, queer, or any other orientation and/or identity?

Are they struggling with depression and anxiety?

Are they self-harming or isolating and shutting you out?

Are you terrified that you won't ask the right questions or be the support they need?

So many questions, I know—and they can either send your heart racing or steel your mind in determination. Few things in this world can strip you to your core like having a child who is struggling or in crisis or worse and having absolutely no idea how to help or support them.

If this resonates with you, you've picked up the right book, and I am so glad you are here. Perhaps you are feeling scared, sad, angry, alone, lost, numb, or overwhelmed. Or perhaps you are happy, relieved, and searching for tools. No matter where you are, I'm sending you a big hug. I can empathize and assure you that whatever you are feeling, even when those feelings are big and uncomfortable, it's okay.

It's more than okay. In fact, you are on a path to incredible beauty, understanding, and enlightenment. Maybe your path has just begun. Your child has just come out to you, and the plethora of feelings and uncertainty about how best to support them is beyond overwhelming. Maybe you are mid-journey and wondering if you will ever know stability again. Regardless of where you are, I am here to tell you there is a light. And you can reach it. Hang on, and just breathe.

If you just rolled your eyes or let out an exasperated sigh, I get it. Parenting is hard. Feeling uncomfortable sucks. Layer in feeling scared or confused or lost or alone, and well, that's just enough to put anyone over the edge. So, express those feelings and read on!

If you're anything like me, you want answers and a plan of action. Maybe you have desperately wished so many times for a magic wand to make it all okay. I know I certainly did. And perhaps, most of all, you'd like a moment of calm and peace so you can catch your breath and regroup. I've been there too. You may feel like you're on an emotional roller coaster. The sleepless nights, the constant knot in your stomach, the fear clenching your heart ever tighter, the inability to think or form a coherent thought mixed with delight that your child is connecting with their authentic self, that they are sharing their thoughts and feelings with you in a new way can be overwhelming. I celebrate and empathize deeply with you. I feel it, even now, as I let myself relive our experience from the beginning.

Here is the key: this is a journey. A journey for your child. A journey for you. A journey together. I am here to tell you that you are not alone. Let love guide you. Allow yourself and your child to pause. Rejoice in the authenticity of the moment, the courage of your child, and the beauty of the road ahead. Let the wise words of A. A. Milne be a mantra: "You are braver than you believe, stronger than you seem, and smarter than you think."

The mission of this book is to provide support, education, and empowerment for anyone who knows and loves an LGBTQ+ child. No one should feel alone. Wrapped up in these pages are ideas to implement, questions to ponder, and tools to help you grow and evolve. You will probably cry, and you might even laugh, but my greatest hope is that you will relate to the stories and research and feel a sense of relief.

. . . . .

In the following pages, you will find transformations within four pillars—simple actions that, when processed and practiced individually, will support you as you move through this journey.

I created the pillars a few years ago when I was brainstorming for my digital course: Learning to Just Breathe. As I sifted through and began to organize all the information, resources, and content I had curated up to that point, a pattern emerged. Four distinct categories became clear. I call these categories *pillars* as they are foundational and they support the family as a whole, as well as each individual.

The first pillar centers around what to do when your child first comes out as LGBTQ+. I remember just wanting to hug Connor, especially when I didn't know what else to say or do. I wanted to take on this new chapter and do all I could to support all of my kids. And so, pillar one, *embrace*, was born.

The second pillar centers around education. This pillar cannot be reached until the first, embrace, is realized. Once you embrace something new, you are open and ready to learn truths and unlearn biases. You need to know where and how to find the best information, resources, and knowledge. Thus, *educate* is a natural second pillar.

The third pillar is the product of the first two pillars and happens as you fully embrace your new reality and learn all you can to support your child—I call this pillar *empower*. Empowering happens as you love and learn and then layer that with experience. Parents and children need to feel empowered to show up authentically in the world, so learning how to be empowered and then how to empower others is crucial.

Finally, the fourth pillar is *love*. Rather than holding equal weight, it is the encapsulation of the other three. Love is really the glue, the magic that holds the other pillars together and magnifies their power. Imagine drawing a heart around the other three pillars. Embrace, educate, and empower cannot occur without love.

Embrace. Educate. Empower. Love.

There is reasoning and flow to practicing the pillars in order. Take your time. If you make a revelation and need to move back a chapter or two, no big deal. There will be opportunities for reflection within each chapter. I invite you to keep a journal with you as you read to work through thoughts and emotions along the way. Look for this symbol and get your pen ready.

As you journal, don't overthink it. Just let your thoughts and feelings flow onto the page. Practice self-compassion, and be gentle with yourself.

At the conclusion of each pillar, there are *action steps* for you to implement. These steps will take what you've learned up to that point and help you not only integrate but also accelerate your learning and growth.

My hope for you is that within the pages of this book, you'll discover helpful information, support, connection, community, empowerment, and love. I hope you experience a sense of relief. I hope you come to know that raising an LGBTQ+ child is a beautiful gift, no matter what your prior experience may be. I hope this book gives you the will to prevail, to advocate, to listen, to learn, to love unconditionally, and to transform.

While humankind, in a very general sense, is becoming more open, affirming, and loving, we all still face different degrees of ugliness and resistance in our daily lives. My broader hope is that this book impacts the world by starting conversations and deepening those already begun. I invite you to join me in being an essential voice in moving things forward.

You are on a dual journey—one of your personal growth and one of your relationship with your child. Just breathe.

It is important to note that as I share the story of our journey, it is through my perspective. While I write with all LGBTQ+ youth in mind, my written reference is to my gay son. I also use "child," but you may substitute "friend" or "loved one" as well. In the instances where I share others' stories and experiences, their names are changed or omitted to protect their privacy.

Let's talk initials before we dive in. You will notice that I use LGBTQ+ throughout this book. There are many versions of this initialism in use, so don't be worried about finding the correct version. I've chosen LGBTQ+ as it is common and accepted. I acknowledge this is an evolving initialism, and we will talk about all the letters included in LGBTQIA+ and what they mean in pillar two.

Till this moment, I never knew myself.

—JANE AUSTEN

My husband, Steve, and I had been looking forward to a couples' weekend at Miraval Spa for months. Being the stay-at-home mom of four kids, I was delighted to get away, and we planned well in advance to make sure it happened. My parents were great about coming to town to watch our kids so we could get time away to be reminded of why we loved—and liked!—each other so much in the first place.

We arrived on the afternoon of February 9, 2017, and for two winter-worn Chicagoans, the dry heat of Arizona was heaven. We spent the afternoon decompressing and enjoying a leisurely dinner with other couples from our group. Steve and I were on our way back to our casita when the call came in.

It was my mom. Frantic. "Heather, I'm so sorry to bother you, but we can't find Connor." I did the time difference math in my head: eleven o'clock in the evening in Arizona was one o'clock in the morning in Chicago. It was a school night, and Connor was sixteen. I felt like I had been kicked in the stomach. Trying to stay calm, I asked, "How long has he been gone? Have you tried his phone?" She launched into the details of hearing him walking around and, upon getting up to check on him, saw that the back door was unlocked and he was nowhere to be found. At this point, he had been gone for over an hour. My thirteen-year-old daughter, Isabelle, was awake as well. They had been calling his phone to no avail, just ringing and ringing. Good news, I thought. That means it's still on.

Meanwhile, Steve had been staring at me, trying to decipher the level of crisis. I hung up with my mom, asking her to sit tight while

I called a few of his friends. I struck out with the first two. The third informed me that he was okay, but she couldn't tell me where he was.

"Can't or won't?" I asked. But she remained firm.

It was at this point that we both began to panic. Connor's location was unavailable on Find My Friends, and he wasn't answering texts or calls from any of us. Even though we live in a relatively quiet suburb, it was now the middle of the night with temperatures in the single digits. To make things worse, this type of behavior was thoroughly unlike him. Connor had always been a rule follower.

My mother was hysterical, my husband was pacing, and I was mere seconds from a full-on panic attack. Heart racing, I left Connor one last voice message and text message letting him know we were calling the police. Lo and behold, within two minutes, he called me back.

I answered, clearly worried but trying to sound calm, "Connor, are you okay?" He was crying. Several seconds passed with no words, only sobs, and terror gripped tighter.

"Mom, I need to tell you something." Several more seconds (or lifetimes) passed. Then, engulfed in an exhale, "I'm gay."

A huge exhale. "Thank God," I exclaimed. "I thought you were dead!" I burst into tears of relief.

"Really?? You're okay with that?" he asked.

"Oh my gosh, yes!" I replied, laughing, yelling, and crying at the same time.

"Just stay on the phone with me until you get home. We'll figure this out!"

I will remember that moment for the rest of my life. The color of the walls in our casita. The smell of the dry Arizona breeze floating in through the open veranda. The vice grip of terror on my heart and the subsequent relief that flooded my body. The tears. Then, feeling so small, so alone, and so completely without a clue what to do next.

We talked as he walked back home, Connor filling me in on the panic attack he'd had that sent him running in the first place. He had fully come to the realization over the prior few months that he was gay, and being home with my parents without us sent him spinning. My parents are very conservative Christians, and Connor was very aware of their beliefs. Every moment he spent with them, protecting his precious secret, crushed him further. He had to run.

It was a wonder that as much as Steve and I had always discussed many topics openly, including sexual orientation and gender identity, he was still scared out of his mind that we would reject him.

We didn't wish to tell my parents at this point, so I just called to let them know that Connor had a panic attack and that he needed kindness and love until we got back home. So much for the relaxing spa weekend.

Steve and I spent the next two days processing, writing down every question that came to mind, and crying.

Please don't misunderstand—neither of us cried because we were upset our son was gay. We cried because we were heartbroken that he had been in so much pain. We cried because our movie reel had changed. Movie reel, you ask? Yes, you know, the one that starts the day your child is born, and you envision what their life will look like. Yep, that movie reel blew up. We cried because we had no idea how to support him. We had entered uncharted territory. Neither of us has gay siblings, and none of our friends had gay children. We live in a community that likes to boast its progressive nature, but suddenly, the monochromatic nature of the area was glaring. Who could we talk to? Would people judge us? Worse, would people judge Connor? We felt alone, confused, and absolutely terrified.

Upon arriving home, I went into a bona fide crisis mode. A highly sensitive person by nature, I'm weirdly extraordinary in a crisis. My strengths trend on the side of emotion and compassion. However, give me a predicament—be it catastrophe, dilemma, or adversity—and I'm on alert and ready to power through. I had a fierce internal struggle raging between my head and my heart: what I was taught growing up versus what I felt to the depth of my soul was right. I needed answers, and I needed them fast.

We sat down with Connor and started asking. There was so much we wanted to know . . . and so much he wanted to tell. How long had he known? Why didn't he tell us sooner? Did any of his friends know? Was he attracted to anyone? Was he sure? (Ugh. Yep . . . we asked.)

All three of us were nervous and scared. Steve and I wanted to reassure Connor that, above all, we loved him and supported him. We wanted to come from a place of curiosity, not judgment. Connor wanted to share his internal struggle and revelation. In theory, it *seemed* easy; the reality was a lot more complicated.

Connor began by telling us that he had known since seventh grade that he was "different" (Connor's word). It took some time to come to terms with it. For three years, he struggled with his identity, his authentic self, loathing what he was coming to terms with—and doing it all alone. Those teenage years are hard enough—add in the realization that you are gay, and you have no one to tell; well, that's just going to result in everything coming out sideways. And it did.

He didn't tell us sooner because he thought we would reject him. This one was a total kick in the gut. Connor and I had always been close. Our family was close. Our home was generally filled with laughter, chaos, sarcasm, and weird conversations. I have subsequently spent many hours on this one. How could he think we would reject him? Why didn't he feel completely safe at home? Had we unwittingly made comments that made him uncomfortable? I'm sure we had—we grew up in the '80s, and our vernacular had not evolved as it should. My heart and soul ache when I think that he genuinely feared rejection from us.

The answer to whether any of his friends knew was yes, only one— the one I called who wouldn't tell me where he was.

His final revelation was that he was not attracted to anyone at school . . . he was attracted to older men (gulp, what?). What did that mean? College older or *older* older? We couldn't even begin to wrap our heads around that one yet.

And, yes, *he was sure.* That we even asked is one of those hindsight moments that we want to kick ourselves for, but in the moment, it came out. We were processing as quickly as possible, wishing to convey love, acceptance, and curiosity. The fact that he had just told us he'd known for three years—*of course* he's sure!—hadn't caught up yet.

Years later, when Connor was a guest on my podcast, *Just Breathe: Parenting Your LGBTQ Teen*, he confirmed that yes, in fact, "Are you sure?" is the most important question NOT to ask.

Once we had some basic questions answered, like any parent trying to process quickly and be parental, we set rules and boundaries. You know, the basics:

1. No dating anyone older than high school age. Those were the rules, gay or straight.
2. Continue therapy. He had just started therapy in January, so he needed to continue those sessions to help him through the coming out process (although, to be fair, at the time, we didn't even know there was a process!).
3. Open communication was a must; otherwise, none of these other rules and boundaries would work.

During those first few weeks of coming to terms with our new reality, we realized our beautiful, firstborn son, ever the rule follower and over-achiever, had been working incredibly hard to remain the kid we thought he was—and worse, who he thought he was *supposed* to be, all the while recognizing that he was not being his authentic self and was terrified to tell us the truth—*for three years.* I am overcome by a deep sadness every time I think about how alone and scared he felt.

It also shed so much light on his ongoing struggle with anxiety and depression. While we were all in a new place with many questions and few answers, at least we had narrowed it down. We could research depression and anxiety in earnest, specifically how LGBTQ+ teens struggle with depression and anxiety and how to support them best. We could also begin our LGBTQ+ education. Goodness, where to start?

Ponder and Reflect

Grab your journal and reflect! Don't overthink it. Just let your thoughts and feelings flow onto the page. Use the following questions as prompts.

- When did you know your child was lesbian, gay, bisexual, transgender, nonbinary, queer, or any other beautiful orientation and/or identity?
- Was there a defining moment?
- Did the door swing wide open with a great whoosh? Or was it just a slow revelation?

Pillar One:
Embrace

*T*here are so many meanings here, and they are all intentional. Embrace the journey, embrace the struggle, embrace the process, embrace the possibilities—but most of all—embrace your child. Holy cow, these humans are extraordinary, unique, beautiful, frustrating, complicated—and perfectly imperfect.

It's helpful to know where you are mentally, emotionally, intellectually, physically, and spiritually as you begin. Take a minute and see which of these statements resonates with you:

1. My child just came out. I'm happy they are expressing their authentic self. I am here to learn more.
2. My child just came out, and I feel nervous about their safety and ill-equipped to be a good support. I am here to learn as much as I possibly can.
3. My child just came out, and I am angry. I do not understand it. It is not what I believe. I am reading this because someone gave it to me.
4. My child has been out for a while, and I want to learn how to be the best support system, become educated, learn how to empower and be empowered, and share this knowledge with others.

There is no wrong answer. You may be a mix of a couple of these, or you may resonate with none of these. The key is that you are completely honest with yourself. Vulnerability and the willingness to unlearn biases and consider the possibilities are the main ingredients for a successful outcome.

Pillar one is all about assessing where you are and where your child is right now. It is also about embracing the journey together, accepting and learning from our mistakes (or things we wish we could do over), and then moving forward.

Of the many things I feel I've botched on this journey, I was delighted to come across the following email in my research and be reminded that I spoke my truth from my heart:

My darling Connor,
    There are so many things I want to say to you and talk with you about. I really wish I were at home.

First, I hope you truly understand now that a mother's love—my love for you—does not have strings attached or requirements. I love you no matter what—unconditionally. It is a love that is so deep and a bond that is very special. It makes my heart hurt to think you doubted that and were so afraid to talk to Dad and me.

Second, if I said anything last night that made you feel guilty or added to your stress and anxiety, I am so very sorry. I (we) were worried and felt so helpless being so far away that I was beside myself with relief when I heard your voice. Hearing you, understanding what you're going through, and getting you the help you need is my only priority.

I love you more than you will ever understand,

Mom

While everyone embarks on a different journey, the elements are similar: learning to embrace the idea of impermanence, allowing our movie reel to explode, becoming comfortable with being uncomfortable, relaxing into the use of humor, and acknowledging fear and overwhelm.

I love this quote by Brené Brown: "Only when we are brave enough to explore the darkness will we discover the infinite power of our light."[1]

Being vulnerable, sharing our struggles and joys as individuals and as a family, and encouraging others to do the same is part of my mission statement and life purpose. Healing from life's wounds, growing from life experience, and celebrating triumph, both personal and of our loved ones, is achieved in part by sharing our stories and seeing ourselves in others. Being vulnerable takes courage, and it also reminds us that we are not alone. Be brave.

CHAPTER ONE

Wrap Your Head Around the News

Once your mind is calm and full of love, there is no room for hatred or fear. Others will trust you because of your open heart.

—DALAI LAMA

So your child has just told you they are lesbian, gay, bisexual, transgender, queer, non-binary, or another sexual orientation or gender identity. Unless this has been obvious for a while, the announcement was probably a bit of a surprise.

The First Feelings and Words

I have found that one of three things immediately happen here, usually subconsciously: The movie reel that you have been keeping in your head—you know, the one that started the day your little one was born, not only recording current events but predicting future ones based on likes and dislikes, habits, personality, etc.—that movie reel explodes. As parents, we are left rather stunned and unsure of what to do next, so in that moment we simply decide to ACCEPT, PANIC, or REJECT.

There are different combinations and expressions of feelings that a parent may have when they learn their child is LGBTQ+. There are a million ways we were raised, different environmental factors (such as where we live, where we work, where our kids go to school, etc.), various access to education, and varying internal factors (such as core beliefs, mental health, spirituality, religion, etc.) which influence our initial reaction.

As I already shared, Steve and I were completely blindsided when Connor came out to us. I cried for days . . . but not for the reasons you may think. I cried because I wasn't physically with him during that moment; because I was beginning to connect all of the dots of his pain; because my movie reel had just exploded; because I had no idea how to help him; because my heart and intuition were in direct conflict with what I learned growing up. It was a lot.

Think about your unique combination of factors and how they influenced your initial reaction. Are these factors fixed or fluid? In other words, are there one or two that are unchangeable, such as how you were raised, where you live, or where your kids go to school? Which ones are more flexible or fluid?

Remember, your child is responding to and processing a lot of feelings too! They are not only dealing with their own challenges, questions, and feelings, but, now that they've shared they are LGBTQ+, they are also dealing with your reactions and emotions.

This is SO important. Please be aware of what you are expressing to your child. It's not their job to manage your feelings. You are both human. Be gentle with where each of you are in this process.

Connor has been a guest on my podcast, *Just Breathe: Parenting Your LGBTQ Teen*, several times. He has shared pieces of his journey, as well as insight into what our teens are thinking and needing from us. I don't think any of us are immune from saying the wrong thing or wishing we knew how to say the right thing, so I asked Connor to share a list of what to say and what not to say. Here are just a few.

WHAT *NOT* TO SAY WHEN YOUR CHILD COMES OUT TO YOU:

- Are you sure?
- This is a lot for me to take in/handle.
- This breaks my heart.
- How do you know?
- You're young; this is probably just a phase.
- We need to have a discussion about this.
- I can't believe my son/daughter/child is gay (or lesbian, bisexual, transgender, queer, or any other sexual orientation or gender identity).
- I always knew you weren't straight.
- I always knew you weren't normal.

DO SAY:

- Thank you for being comfortable enough to share that with me.
- That takes a lot of courage.
- I'm proud of you.
- I see you.
- My love for you is unconditional; this changes nothing.
- How can I best support you in this process?
- Is this something you've shared with others? I don't want to say anything to anyone you haven't told yet.

The only way forward is to be willing to be curious. Curiosity is the antidote to judgment. You do not have to agree to accept, but to move to the next pillar, you do need to have the desire to understand your child's sexual orientation and/or gender identity.

This first step may take a few hours, a few days, or a few months. Take the time now to process. This is not a sprint; it's a journey. And a journey implies a long and winding trip.

Being in an authentic relationship with someone else requires you to be in an authentic relationship with yourself first. You may uncover a few limiting beliefs or peel back a few layers you didn't realize were there. Take your time. You are learning to embrace!

Open Your Heart and Mind

The first days, weeks, and months after Connor came out were messy. Or, more accurately, each of us was a mess in our own unique way. Connor's struggle with accepting himself and self-loathing increased by the day, and the learning curve was akin to traversing a treacherous mountain pass. Every time Steve and I thought we had caught up or figured something out, another challenge or struggle was added. We had no idea at the time how deep Connor's self-loathing and desperation ran nor what he was willing to do to escape it.

I was my own kind of mess. At the most inconvenient moments—in front of the middle school principal, at the Starbucks drive-thru window, mid-conversation with a random neighbor—I would lose my internal battle, and the tears would come. Not the pretty kind, either. The lump in your throat, blotchy face, mascara-ruining kind. Sometimes I knew the tears were coming from being overwhelmed, worried, or stressed; other times, I think the tears were a combination of all the above plus every emotion I absorbed from my kids and husband.

I eventually ran out of the energy to keep myself pulled together, and something quite magical occurred. Rather than finding myself in the fetal position, not being able to function, I found freedom: freedom to mourn the change in our movie reel; freedom to experience my feelings and then let them go; freedom to heal and grow and move forward.

This freedom took time to understand. And it took work. I realize now that this was when my heart and mind began to open fully. It was an accelerator through the stages of mourning, not just of our movie reel but of decades-old traumas and relationship reveals.

Dipping my toe in the pool of vulnerability allowed me to begin to let go of my *if I look good on the outside, I will feel good on the inside* coping mechanism. I discovered that being vulnerable and authentic with my kids, with Steve, and with others not only lifted the massive weight of perfection from my shoulders but also allowed others a safe space in which to be vulnerable. This was a HUGE revelation for all of us!

Initially, this work was only part of the shifting Steve, Connor, and I were doing, but over time, it encompassed all six of us. We learned how to peel back the layers, let go of prior expectations, and unlearn biases. We could express how we felt without judgment. We could be messy around each other and know we are still loved unconditionally. We could verbally process or take a pause and just be allowed to *be*. NO WAY!! These were all such profound mental and emotional shifts, and we soaked them in until our dehydrated souls were overflowing.

I realize that if, before I was ready, someone had said to me, "Heather, you need to transform (or evolve) your thinking completely to have an authentic relationship with your husband or your kids," I would have either lashed out in anger or shut down and retreated. That was about the extent of my emotional intelligence at the time. So, I understand if you are reading this with resistance. All I'm asking is that you open your heart and your mind to the possibility. There isn't a deadline. This isn't a competition. This is your journey with yourself, your child, and your family. You get to write it your way!

Take a moment and think about your journey so far with your child and with your family. Are there particular moments that you remember with clarity? Are they moments of revelation? Transformation? Celebration? Or even "Wow, I wish I could do that over!" These are all of the pieces that make this journey uniquely yours.

It takes time to pull apart our unique concoction of baggage that is keeping us stuck—whether it is our core beliefs, childhood programming, or social pressure (or a combination thereof). This is not a linear process. Focus on one positive action, one authentic conversation, or one moment without the vice-grip of fear. Give yourself permission to take the smallest of steps, one at a time, until you are ready for the next. Allow the possibility of a new perspective. This is how evolution and growth occur.

The elements needed to open your heart and your mind are similar and fall into four categories:

EMBRACE THE IDEA OF IMPERMANENCE

Impermanence is the concept that all situations and feelings last for a limited time. Whether you think of this in terms of seasons or ebbs and flows, know that whatever you are experiencing is only for a moment in time. Happiness, delight, love, contentedness, sadness, despair, and grief are all in a constant state of flow. You cannot hold tighter to make one stay or wish harder to make one leave. You can manifest by shifting your thoughts and actions.

The word "IMPERMANENCE" was Connor's first tattoo, and it is still my favorite. He doesn't love it the way he used to, but even that is a powerful example of the word. What a great reminder.

BECOME COMFORTABLE WITH BEING UNCOMFORTABLE

It is human nature to shrink away from or dislike anything that feels uncomfortable. Many times, discomfort accompanies new information, new routines, or even a new item, such as a car or refrigerator.

This may feel a bit daunting at first. Become aware of the information, the routines, or the situations that bring you discomfort. Now, sit with that information. Don't try to solve it or figure it out or pretend it doesn't exist. Merely sit with it. Practice this each time discomfort comes up for you. You may choose to journal about it as well. This is one of the most significant shifts I can teach you. Not only will it help you with your child, but it will also help you in all aspects of your life.

Before I became aware of this, l would become frozen in uncomfortable situations. I didn't know how to express my feelings and just wanted to curl up and make the discomfort disappear. Once I was able to name it, understand it, and realize that sitting with that awful, uncomfortable feeling was actually helping me grow and shift, that was a game-changer! **Name it to tame it!** So, I am naming it for you, and, you guessed it, naming and sitting with your discomfort will be part of your journaling at the end of this chapter.

One last note on being uncomfortable—when I consider trying something new, and I feel uncomfortable, nine times out of ten, I know it is a sign that I should absolutely embrace it and move through it!

USE HUMOR AS A WAY TO PROCESS

This is the fun one! For better or worse, my go-to in high-stress situations tends to be humor, and it is Steve's as well. Typically, we're pretty good about reading whomever we're dealing with to know if they can handle humor, but every so often, we're off. If you're thinking, *Are you crazy? I'm so worried or stressed all of the time; how can I possibly be funny or use humor?* Don't let this stress you out too! It is a tool you gradually relax into. For me, it is taking small daily happenings and over-dramatizing them or under-dramatizing them and then sprinkling them with self-deprecation in a way that I know will make the other person laugh. I kind of tripped upon this method of processing and found that as I talked and laughed through different crises, it was easier to work through and figure out the situation at hand. I know, weird, but worth trying. Whether you are witty, excel at sarcasm and self-deprecation, or share humor best through simple jokes, funny stories, or memes, humor can be your saving grace.

You will trip up, and that's okay—I have made my own share of blunders in my attempts. Luckily for me, Steve and all four of my kids have quick-witted, often hysterically funny personalities, so using humor to diffuse or just create a relaxed atmosphere is, thankfully, a breeze at home.

ACKNOWLEDGE FEAR AND OVERWHELM

I know, this one can be tough. Like feeling uncomfortable, it is human nature to allow fear to stop us in our tracks. Both fear and overwhelm can freeze us and make our minds go blank. They can make our minds spin with worse-case scenarios and what-ifs. Our fight or flight response doesn't discern between acute danger (in which the reaction of fear is warranted) and fear triggered as a reaction to non-life-threatening information or fear of the future.

So, the way to counteract this natural response is with acknowledgment and awareness. Try saying, "I see you fear. I feel you too. I know you are trying to protect me, but I've got this; you can stand down." It may feel silly at first, but it sends a powerful message to your brain and body that a mentally and physically freezing surge of cortisol is not necessary. It is another way to employ the name-it-to-tame-it method!

Ponder and Reflect

Grab your journal and reflect! Don't overthink it. Just let your thoughts and feelings flow onto the page.

- Try the name-it-to-tame-it method. You can say it silently to yourself, or you can write it down. Name your biggest fear right now, describe it, and list all the feelings and physical sensations it brings up for you. Take that breath; give yourself a moment.
- Is there anything you feel discomfort around or fearful about? Write about that, reflect, allow yourself time. I am serious when I say to sit through the discomfort and then come back and do it all again until you feel a shift in your heart and mind.
- What does having an open heart and mind look and feel like to you?
- Visualize being in that state.
- Are you ready to learn how to embrace this journey with your child?
- How does that make you feel? Be honest.

CHAPTER TWO

Get Yourself Grounded

Get yourself grounded, and you can navigate even the
stormiest roads in peace.

—STEVE GOODIER

et yourself grounded. Get centered. Breathe. Become calm.
What do those statements mean to you? How do they make
you feel? Do you have any routines or practices in place that
allow you the space to find and feel like the best version of yourself?
The place where you're open to receiving new information, where you
can see and hear your child, where your cup is at least half full and perhaps even full and overflowing?

The goal is to be in a place mentally, physically, emotionally, and
spiritually where you can authentically embrace your child's coming
out process and be prepared to learn and grow.

If the cup analogy is new to you, think of your cup as your source
of energy, love, patience—all the things we give to those around us.
When that cup is full, we can handle almost anything that is thrown
our way. We can listen and be present, we can respond thoughtfully
when needed, and we can validate and problem solve (when asked!).
You know exactly what it feels like when the opposite is true, right?

You literally feel depleted and empty. You have no patience; you're likely short-tempered or sharp-tongued; you're exhausted. It takes a conscious effort to refill our cup, and it is done by creating a purposeful self-care routine.

If you're thinking, "but there is so much chaos going on around me," or "my focus needs to be 100 percent on my child—I don't have time for a shower, let alone a self-care routine!" I completely hear you. I offer this encouragement as someone who literally became mentally, physically, and emotionally sick because I pushed myself to the extreme. I didn't understand that being self**less** was actually self**ish**.

So, yes, in a book about loving your LGBTQ+ child, there is information on loving yourself too.

Self-Care

Self-care looks different for each one of us. For me, self-care is having a little time to myself—uninterrupted—when I can feed my mind, body, and soul what they need at that moment. It could be a walk with my dogs, practicing yoga or kickboxing (depending on what type of energy I need to cultivate or release), taking extra time to pamper my skin, doing my nails, reading a novel, or even playing Words With Friends. My ultimate go-to practice for grounding is meditation and breathing exercises.

If this is new to you, or if you struggle to connect with what self-care and grounding look like for you, don't worry! As we shift from an age of mentally and physically working ourselves to the bone while depriving our minds, souls, and hearts of any nourishment or care, proceeding with gentleness is most important. This is a practice that will take time, and it is a practice that will reward you tenfold!

Here are a few self-care practices that are good for all of us to include.

SLEEP

There is no denying that restful and restorative sleep can genuinely make everything look brighter. Hundreds of studies on top of each of our personal experiences prove this. The trick is making it a priority—turning off our phones or the TV or putting down that really good book before we hit that place of sheer exhaustion. A bedtime routine to prepare your body to repair and restore fully is of equal importance to the morning routine that prepares you for the day ahead. I empathize with those who struggle with this one because there is always one more thing to do. I tend to push myself into that late-night second wind just to get a few minutes of peace, too, but I am actively working on it and can always tell a huge difference when I am successful.

STAY HYDRATED

Again, an obvious one, and one that is mentioned everywhere you look. Being well hydrated literally affects every system in your body, as well as your mood and ability to think and process clearly. The good news is that you can accomplish this in many ways throughout the day.

While water is the best choice, I know that it can get a little dull, so here are a few ideas: add lemon, cucumber, or fruit to your water; in the winter, heat your water and add lemon and raw honey; try herbal teas (hot or cold); or consider bubbly waters—there are a million of them out there now. Essentially, you just want to stay away from caffeine and added sugar. There are scores of apps like HidrateSpark or Waterllama to help you stay on track.

MOVE YOUR BODY EVERY DAY!

We all know that exercise is good for us, but with everything else going on, sometimes it is hard to stay consistent (or even do at all)! If you do not have an exercise routine, don't fret! Start small and do what feels good to you. The goal is to move your body.

- yoga or stretching to start the day
- get up from your desk every ninety minutes and walk up and down the stairs or stretch your shoulders, neck, and back (ragdoll pose is a fabulous yoga pose that you can use here!)
- walk outside through a nearby park (being in nature is the best way to ground)

- dancing while you cook (just move and get your blood flowing!)

Have any of these resonated with you? Are you already making a mental list of tiny shifts you can make to take care of yourself?

MEDITATE

One of the things I love about meditation is that you can find a guided session for literally everything! I've been meditating for several years, and I go back and forth between guided sessions that are specific to my mental/emotional/spiritual space at that moment and silent meditation. Sometimes it is so grounding to sit quietly with soft music and allow my whole body to calm down and just breathe.

Meditation is incredibly personal and accessible to everyone regardless of belief system. One of the many beauties of meditation is that you can meditate on the floor, in a chair, on the couch, under a tree, or on the beach. There are no rules! Finally, for all of you who believe that meditation is not for you because you can't sit still or you can't quiet your mind, I have fabulous news: *You don't need to sit still or clear your mind of all thoughts!*

Removing this piece of misinformation about meditation was a game-changer for me!

You can meditate while walking or gardening. You can meditate while biking, painting, or playing an instrument. The practice isn't about making yourself have no thoughts (that's just an exercise in futility!); the practice of meditation is about awareness. Notice the thoughts, and let them go. Notice your breath. Notice the sensations around you.

Here are my favorite (free!) meditation apps:

- Calm
- Headspace
- Gabby Bernstein
- Chopra

Each of these has guided meditations, sleep stories, and all styles of music and nature sounds to help you meditate. Remember, you can start with five minutes! And ANYONE can meditate.

When you're ready to level up, add mantras or affirmations to your meditation practice. You can write them down and hang them in your office, bathroom, kitchen, or wherever you find them most effective. The great thing is that while you can google mantras or affirmations by famous people, you will connect most intimately with the ones you create for yourself. Here are a few of mine:

- I am worthy.
- I am enough; I am complete.
- I feel supported and loved.
- I see possibilities, not limitations.
- I have abundance in all ways, spiritual, love, friendship, knowledge, and finances.
- I speak my truth.
- I listen to my intuition.
- I release all emotions and responsibilities that are not mine.

BREATHE

Understanding our breathing unlocks a treasure trove of coping mechanisms, stress relief strategies, and a plethora of other benefits. There are four specific types of breathing I share here but know that there are many more iterations, as well as specific breathing that you can do for specific needs.

The first one is called **resonant breathing**. Also known as coherent breathing, it is simply taking five full breaths in one minute, which calms your nervous system. According to Healthline, "Breathing at this rate maximizes your heart rate variability (HRV), reduces stress, and, according to one 2017 study, can reduce symptoms of depression when combined with Iyengar yoga."[1] (Iyengar yoga is unique for its precision of alignment, sequence of asanas, and use of props.)

Here's how to use resonate breathing:

- Inhale for a count of five.
- Exhale for a count of five.
- Repeat cycle for one full minute.
- Tip: close your eyes if possible to help you focus on your breath.

Next up is **alternate nostril breathing**. This one definitely takes a little practice. Don't worry if one nostril is easier to breathe out of than the other. That is normal. Training your body to breathe in and out from your nose will increase the air passageways over time and make this easier. Alternate nostril breathing is excellent for relaxing, improving lung function, boosting cardiovascular function, and lowering heart rate.

Here's how to do it:

- Find a comfortable seated position. This technique requires more focus, so it is best to practice in a place without distractions.
- Take your right hand, press your first and middle fingers toward your palm, and extend your other fingers.
- Exhale, and then use your right thumb to gently close your right nostril.
- Inhale through your left nostril and then close your left nostril with your right pinky and ring fingers.
- Lift your thumb and exhale out through your right nostril.
- Inhale through your right nostril and then close this nostril.
- Lift your fingers to open your left nostril and exhale through this side.
- This is one cycle.
- Continue this breathing pattern for up to five minutes.

Box breathing is a great technique that can be used anywhere to stay calm and focused; it is especially useful in stressful situations.

Here's how to use box breathing:

- Inhale to a count of five.
- Hold for five.
- Exhale to a count of five.
- Hold for five.
- Repeat five times.

Finally, **4-7-8 breathing**, also known as *relaxing breath*, involves breathing in for four seconds, holding the breath for seven seconds, and exhaling for eight seconds. This breathing pattern reduces anxiety and helps you fall asleep.

Here's how to do it:

- Completely exhale through your mouth, making a whoosh or heavy sigh sound.
- Close your mouth and quietly inhale through your nose to a mental count of four.
- Hold your breath for a count of seven.
- Exhale through your mouth, making a whoosh sound for a count of eight.
- Repeat as needed.

Try each of these to see if any resonate with you.

There are many more variations out there and many fabulous (free!) breathing apps you can try. Do your own search to find what you like. Here are a few of my favorites to get you started:

- The Breathing App
- iBreathe
- Paced Breathing
- Breathe (this one is great if you have an Apple Watch)

Integrate these self-care practices (sleep, hydrate, move your body, meditate, and breathe) and note what works best for you. Take some time to think about what you need mentally, physically, emotionally, and spiritually to feel calm and grounded in your life. There is no wrong answer!

The Value of a Pause

We still live in a society where *doing* and *going* are rewarded. In recent years, *being* and *pausing* have gained recognition as equal states or actions, so talking about and practicing them is essential. Think about when you feel most connected to yourself or when you come up with your best ideas. Is it when you are multitasking and moving a million miles an hour? Or is it when you're fully present, grounded, and have taken a moment to pause?

Everything we've talked about in this chapter lends itself to the value of pausing. When you pause, everything works better. You can think and make decisions better. You can breathe and move better. Your emotions are calmer. You are connected to yourself, your higher self, and your spiritual realm.

Ponder and Reflect

Grab your journal and reflect! Don't overthink it. Just let your thoughts and feelings flow onto the page.

- Do you have a self-care routine or ritual?
- If not, what activities or rituals calm you or get you in a space where you feel like the best version of yourself?
- Recount a moment in time when you actively paused. How did it change what was going on around you?

Sleep, staying hydrated, moving your body, meditation, and breathing exercises are the five areas of self-care I touched on.

- Which of these (if any) appeal to you as a way to fill your cup?
- What else would you add?
- Make a list of two more activities or rituals that soothe you or get you to that place where you can handle anything that comes your way.

CHAPTER THREE

Tell Your Kid You Love Them

Speak with your children as if they are the wisest, kindest, most beautiful humans on earth, for what they believe is what they will become.

—BROOKE HAMPTON

This may seem relatively simple at first glance. You may be thinking, "Tell my kids that I love them. Of course, I love them!" Just hang in here with me.

You may already be halfway through a mental list of all of the reasons you love your kids, as well as every little thing you have ever done for them since the day they were born. I get it! As parents, we show so much of our love and care through actions from the moment we hold these little ones in our arms for the first time until, well, forever, right? And actions are a beautiful way to truly show how much we love or care for someone.

While we have likely whispered "I love you" a million times, it is when they are toddlers and younger children that we show our love through both words and actions as we teach our kids the concepts of love, kindness, connection, and so on. At this age, they soak up the I-love-yous and hugs like crazy—and often ask for more!

By the preteen years, the beginnings of their massive physical, mental, and emotional growth is evident. They may begin to brood or show moodiness or try some colorful language or ask questions you've never heard from them before. Still, they accept hugs and often return an "I love you."

And then, BAM, the teen years hit.

THIS is why I wrote this chapter. If we took what our teenagers throw at us for face value, we might genuinely believe they want nothing to do with us, and we would spend our days wondering how we became the dumbest humans on earth overnight. However, this could not be further from the truth! Trust me on this. In the midst of this massive change, they are figuring out who they are, how they see the world, and what they may want to do with their lives. College? Career? Job-training? Travel? They are also starting the natural process of pulling away from us in their later teen years as they prepare to leave the nest.

Let Them *Hear* Your Love

There is no more critical time to verbally tell your kid that you love them—for who they are right now, at this moment in time. This is so important I am going to repeat it—**tell your kid that you love them for who they are right now, at this moment in time**.

It is important for all kids to hear those powerful words—I love you—and to feel seen and valued. However, I believe it is crucial for our LGBTQ+ kids, no matter where they are in their coming out process. In the moments that we see them struggle, our natural, loving parent desire is to soothe—and in doing so, may focus on their potential or who they are growing into being or the future.

Don't get me wrong—it is good—and essential for your child's self-esteem to hear you share your positive thoughts about their potential. But if we only focus on this future version (which may not even be accurate or shared), we send the message that who they are right now is not enough.

- I share this because I am guilty of it. And many other parents have shared similar stories to mine. I will never forget Connor telling us that the message to him was he wasn't okay. He felt like we were focusing on some future version of him that may be way off base, and that was adding pressure and expectations to an already vulnerable and fragile human. My heart still hurts when I think about this, but I am also grateful that he could articulate this so that we could make the necessary shifts.

- When Connor was going through really rough patches, which he did on and off for three years, Steve and I would immediately try to fix the problem or help him feel better by telling him he would be okay, or he was smart, or life would get better. What he needed was validation that we really saw him, that we heard the messages in his words—or at least asked for clarification when we didn't understand. He needed to know that we were holding space for him and loving him unconditionally as he worked through the shame, the self-loathing, and the search for an answer to that all-important question: "Who am I?"

Understanding Connor's needs provided SO MANY LESSONS! And it was in that understanding and those lessons that many of our positive shifts occurred that brought profound connection and initiated healing.

So, what was our first shift? We first needed to learn to sit with that awful, uncomfortable feeling that comes when we're in the process of learning new information, unlearning biases, or figuring out how to connect with and support our LGBTQ+ child instead of trying to fix or soothe with a platitude. Our second shift was restructuring our language and learning to be aware of the power and message of words. In this case, it meant telling Connor *how much we love him, who he is, right now, at this moment in time.*

Each and every one of our kids needs this simple, yet deeply meaningful, assurance!

Now, they are still adolescents and teens, so don't expect outward rejoicing when you get it right. However, I promise you they are soaking it up on the inside. And you will see the reflection of their internal joy in their behavior.

Be patient with yourself and with your child. Most of what I am sharing and teaching are shifts that occur over time, not overnight fixes.

There are dozens of ways to tell your child that you love them. In addition to saying those three beautiful words, the following actions allow you to mix things up while still conveying that all-important message.

- **Listen to them.** Put down your phone or turn away from your computer or TV and make eye contact. Body language speaks volumes.
- **Validate them.** This lets them know they have been seen and heard. More on how to do this is in chapter thirteen.
- **Ask questions about things they are interested in.** You may be surprised!
- **Do an activity that they love.** For example, if they love art, spend an afternoon walking through local galleries together.
- **Make their favorite meal and offer silent love and support.** If they are feeling stressed but are either struggling to articulate why or are keeping it all in, the way to their heart may be food or simply letting them know you are there for them.

The idea is that you connect with them and let them know how loved they are in as many ways as you possibly can.

Opening the Doors of Communication

Regardless of where your child is in the coming out process, my guess is you have been spinning a bit, trying to sort through dozens of your own thoughts and feelings, as well as trying to understand your child. Where you are right now likely depends on three factors:

1. How open you are.
2. How open your child wants to be or feels they can be with you.
3. How open your child perceives you to be.

I know the last one isn't fair, but it is the reality. So, opening pathways to better and more effective communication is rather crucial to move forward.

Before you start freaking out, breathe. I'm not saying all communication struggles need to be solved. I'm saying that the doors for communication need to be open at least a crack, and obstructions or barriers need to be cleared.

Obstructions or barriers can be verbal and non-verbal, they can be conscious and subconscious, or they can be physical. One example is reaching a point where you have locked horns with your teen and both think you are right. Another example of an obstruction or barrier is residual hurt or resentment from past conversations that creates instant tension or defensiveness.

So what can we do to clear any obstructions or barriers and create effective, connected communication with our children? Gary Gilles, LCPC, suggests the following:

- Listen with your whole body. This means make eye contact, face your child, and point your feet toward them—doing this signals to them on a psychological level that you are present and listening.
- Acknowledge your child's feelings and try to see the situation through their eyes or through their lens of experience.
- Teach your children that they have options and that there are choices in every decision. This is especially helpful when the two of you disagree. Encourage your children to be part of the solution by articulating what they want or what they would like to see happen.[1]

As the parent, you need to set the tone and accept and learn from your mistakes (or the things we wish we could do over). You don't need long, complicated conversations. Instead, make a simple statement like "I'm here, and I want to understand you," or "I realize that you have been struggling, and I want to support you." If you are struggling with the news yourself, be honest and say something to the effect of "I am struggling with the fact that you are (fill in the blank), but that is on me to figure out, and I am willing to do that." All of these statements can be followed up with: "I want to move forward; would you be willing to move forward with me?"

Here are a few more suggestions for meaningful questions that may initiate conversations:

- "What do you need from us?"
- "What about being out makes you most happy?"
- "What about coming out makes you the most scared or nervous?"

Again, as much as they may be pushing back on the outside—giving an attitude, rolling eyes, crossing arms, or otherwise throwing angst your way—remember that a positive connection with you is very important to them. Teenage angst, so to speak, can be so hurtful and may require moments of biting your tongue, but roll yourself in Teflon and know that I, and so many others in this community, are cheering you on—you are not alone. Take a deep breath and dig deep for your own version of the statements you know will resonate with your child. Embrace that you will make mistakes, and that is okay. Acknowledge them, own them, and try again.

Ponder and Reflect

Grab your journal and reflect! Don't overthink it. Just let your thoughts and feelings flow onto the page.

- Take some time over the next few weeks to slow down long enough to notice a moment or a conversation with your teen.
- Note words you may use or the times you feel uncomfortable and sit through it.

· · · · ·

Remember, feeling uncomfortable is okay—growth is occurring. This allows us to truly reflect on what is working and where we need to shift.

CHAPTER FOUR

Surrender to Embrace

The journey is learning that pain, like love, is simply
something to surrender to.

—GLENNON DOYLE

L earning to embrace is a lot more complex than you may have
first thought, but I promise it is worth the work. Just look at
how far you've come already! You've at least begun the process
of wrapping your head around the news. You've learned the basics of
how to get yourself grounded and are practicing different techniques
to see what feels best for you. And, you've learned why it's vital to tell
your kid(s) you love them.

What Does it Mean to Surrender?

The final step of the first pillar is to *surrender*. The concept of surrender can be complicated and perplexing because it looks different
for each one of us. Answer the following questions for yourself. (I have
listed some possible answers to get you started.)

- **What am I surrendering to?** [pain, love, helplessness, overwhelm, fear]
- **How do I think I will experience surrender?** [emotionally,
spiritually, mentally, physically]

- **What do I hope to accomplish by surrendering?** [the ability
  to embrace others, the ability to connect or let go]

It has taken courage and resolve on your part to arrive here. You can do this. I promise that when you put the time and thought into this process, the freedom and clarity you will find on the other side is worth every minute of mental and emotional labor.

There are many types of psychological surrender—emotional, spiritual, and mental. What I am sharing with you is rather a potpourri of all I have learned, what worked for my family and me, and what has worked for my clients. The way each of us approach surrendering is specific to the journey we are on with our child or loved one, and it is an important component of learning to embrace.

The approach to surrender that I have created has three stages—mourning or grieving, vulnerability, and evolution.

Allow Mourning or Grieving

We typically think of mourning or grieving when it pertains to the loss of a loved one, a family member, a friend, or even a pet. However, experiencing grief and mourning applies to any loss: the loss of a relationship, the loss of a job, the loss of a home, the loss of a dream. Mourning or grieving is the first of the three stages of surrender.

The movie reel analogy occurred to me very early in our journey. I was sitting with Connor's high school advisor and was struck by the accuracy as it came out of my mouth. I think it seemed profound at the time because I was a hot mess of emotion, and describing how I was feeling with the movie reel analogy may have been the only succinct few sentences I put together. It was the perfect description of how I was experiencing the upside-down blur that was my life. I have subsequently shared it with clients and friends alike, and it is a light bulb moment every time.

From the moment our babies enter this world, the movie reel begins. It remains largely unseen, even part of the subconscious, as data and snapshots of time are added. Information is collected, such as what toys they liked to play with as toddlers, their favorite color in kindergarten, what activities they enjoyed throughout childhood and into adolescence, who their friends were, and how they interacted with them. All of this information is compiled in the background to create the theme of the movie reel. Now, here is the important part. As parents, we take this information and project their future—if and where they may go to college, what they will major in, what job they will have, who they will marry, etc. Since we live in a heteronormative society where the assumption and guiding belief that everyone is heterosexual and that heterosexuality is superior to all other sexualities, the default assumption is still that our child will marry someone of the opposite sex.

When our kids come out to us, as adolescents especially, that movie reel explodes. We suddenly become hyper-aware of OUR assumptions and plans for our child. In that moment, those plans are eviscerated, and as the million pieces of what you thought might be settle all around you, the place they previously occupied may be replaced with fear and overwhelm.

Now, if you already had a feeling about your child's sexual orientation or gender identity before they came out to you, your experience may have been a bit different. It is also possible that your mindset has always been very open to all of the possibilities, so having your child share that they are gay, bisexual, or gender diverse is just another day in your household.

I honor and validate your experience wherever it falls on the spectrum of possibilities.

If you do align more with the first experience of surprise, it is vitally important to allow yourself time to process and mourn your movie reel. This does not make you a bad parent. It makes you human. This must be done in order to move forward, and it must be done alone. This is not to say you can't work it through with your partner or friend or therapist—**you cannot, however, under any circumstances, dump it all on your child. It is not their responsibility to hold your hand**. Additionally, they are processing their own feelings and experiences, whether it is mourning their movie reel or feeling excited or curious about the endless possibilities ahead of them.

Allow Vulnerability

Allowing yourself to be vulnerable is a critical component of mourning and grieving, as well as the second stage in surrendering to embrace. Vulnerability is so important that it plays a part in all three stages. I attribute this to the fact that allowing ourselves to be vulnerable can be quite uncomfortable or scary, but once we break through that threshold, watch out! I realize that the fact that these stages flow together and are not neat boxes on their own may be enough to create discomfort. Take a breath. This is intentional.

Vulnerability has gotten a bad rap and, in previous generations, was seen as a weakness. However, like with so many things, we are beginning to understand that vulnerability requires strength, courage, resiliency, creativity, resolve, and intelligence. Vulnerability is the opposite of weakness.

Once we let go of the barriers and the fears that prevent us from being vulnerable, we can be introspective. We can explore WHY certain beliefs and biases exist around sexuality and gender identity.

It absolutely can be alarming to peel back the layers and do the work to unlearn, but holy cow, is it worth it! On the other side, you will feel like you are seeing everything through a new light, one filled with possibilities and the freedom to embrace. Allowing yourself to be vulnerable may also give you the space and awareness to acknowledge that you don't have all the answers. In fact, it conversely may take the pressure off you to feel like you *need* to know all the answers! Being vulnerable with our kids gives them permission to do so as well and opens the doors to more authentic communication.

Allow Evolution

This final stage of surrender may take considerably more time than the first two. As you uncover each layer, you will find that you are navigating and living in the space of discomfort between old beliefs, thought patterns, and behaviors and new beliefs, thought patterns, and behaviors. Integrating forgiveness, resilience, and mindfulness as you peel back each layer will support your process. As you learn about these principles, be gentle with yourself. Stop and allow yourself a moment of celebration in the moments that are ridiculously uncomfortable. You are doing hard things to be a better human!

FORGIVENESS

One practice that has become extremely helpful in my evolution is forgiveness. My lifelong understanding of forgiveness was that it was about the other person. In other words, if someone said or did something to hurt me, forgiveness was saying, "It's okay, I absolve you of all accountability." Does that sound familiar? Well, you can imagine how my mind was blown to discover that, in fact, forgiveness is about letting go. The person, people, or idea that caused harm have no active involvement.

For example, I forgive my brother for his unkind words toward Connor, the LGBTQ+ community, and our family because I want to let go and move forward. I want to stop ruminating and waiting for an apology. Another example involves a client of mine. Through the process of evolution, she was able to forgive her mother for not accepting or affirming her gay son. This act of forgiveness allowed her to let go of the anger, the expectation, and the hurt and to move forward with a lightness and joy that she had never experienced before.

The idea is to forgive and eliminate any blame that is being held in your mind, body, or soul. Let it purge itself from every cell of your body. This allows healing to begin and your beautiful evolution to continue.

RESILIENCE

Resilience is a learned trait that will support you on your evolutionary journey. We know that we become resilient by experiencing and learning from challenges. But what are other ways we can build resilience? The University of California Berkeley's science-based *Greater Good Magazine* shares science-based ideas for resilience including change the narrative, practice self-compassion, and meditate:[1]

- **Change the narrative.** Practicing this tactic taps into the powerful practice of understanding that you cannot change other people, but you can change the way you respond to them. Add to that the practice of awareness. When you recognize that a particular situation has you frozen or spinning, pause for a moment and consider your other response options.

- **Practice self-compassion.** In other words, be gentle with yourself. If you fall into the harshly self-critical camp, know that you are not alone and that self-compassion is the antidote. Yes, it takes practice. This is a habit or defense mechanism that took years to build. When you make a mistake or feel "I should" creeping in, take a deep breath and say something kind to yourself, such as "I am enough." It will feel awkward at first, like anything new, but keep at it. You will find the language that feels right to you and perhaps even add in other practices that allow you to be gentle with yourself!

- **Meditate.** Most simply and most powerfully, meditation helps you stay in the present. Fear and anxiety are based on the past and future, two places we have no control over. We have this moment. Find a meditation practice that works for you. Meditating daily is an action you can begin today to help you strengthen your resilience. Staying in the present will help you with changing your response and self-compassion. One helps build and strengthen the other. You've got this!

MINDFULNESS

Practicing mindfulness is the final practice I want to share that will support and strengthen you as you evolve. The awareness and observation involved in mindfulness are practices of one who is quite advanced on their evolutionary journey, so big hugs and high fives—you are doing such good work! Because I am one who loves tips and action items, here are three of my favorite ways to practice mindfulness.

BEGIN THE DAY WITH A MINDFUL PRACTICE

The morning routine sets the tone for the entire day. Try adding a few of the following practices into your morning routine to begin weaving mindfulness into your life.

- Upon waking and before getting out of bed, take three long belly breaths.
- Ask the question: What can I do today to show up for the highest good of everyone, including myself? This can be posed to yourself, God, the universe, or your spirit guides.
- Enjoy that sacred first cup of coffee (or morning beverage of choice) in stillness and silence, allowing space and time for your senses to awaken.
- Spend a few minutes writing in your journal. It can be free writing or gratitude. The most important thing is to be present.
- Is there a gentle movement practice that you enjoy? Yoga or a walk are lovely ways to round out your morning routine.

Check in with yourself throughout the day.

LEARN TO PAUSE

Have you ever driven somewhere and once you arrived had no recollection of how you got there? Wild and a little bit scary! This and so many other repetitive tasks happen throughout our days because our brain essentially goes on auto-pilot. The short answer to why this happens is that our brain performs millions of functions every day, and when it recognizes one on repeat, it takes the extra *aware* energy from that task and applies it somewhere else. It is both good and harmless to interrupt this function of the brain by pausing and pulling ourselves back into the present. Acknowledge the activity that your brain put on auto-pilot, and create a new pattern. Choose something that involves an action, such as leaving yourself a variety of Post-it notes. Pausing creates mindfulness.

PRACTICE MINDFUL EATING

Eating can easily be another auto-pilot activity. I'm certainly guilty of it, especially lunch, which I typically eat at my desk while working. Not surprisingly, there are a plethora of physical, mental, and spiritual health benefits to mindful eating. Aside from *don't eat at your desk*, here are a few more tips to help you taste and enjoy your meals, as well as strengthen your mindfulness skills.

- Sit in a place without distractions (i.e., TV, computer, phone).
- Employ ALL of your senses. Taste may be center stage, but think about what you see, feel, and smell.
- Chew your food and take a breath in between bites. Not only does this help with the enjoyment factor, it also allows time for your stomach to tell your brain that it is full.

Mourning, allowing yourself to be vulnerable, and evolving allow for so much growth. Truly surrendering provides us the space to embrace the people we love, the greater community, and all activities we engage in as our *true* selves.

Ponder and Reflect

Grab your journal and reflect! Don't overthink it. Just let your thoughts and feelings flow onto the page.

- Write an honest assessment of where you and your child are **right now.**
- Where would you like to be **in the future**?
- Reflect on your thoughts on the three stages: allow mourning, allow vulnerability, and allow evolution.
- Explore ways to surrender, as well as uncover why there may be a struggle in doing so.
- Journal about one goal you have around surrendering.

Action Steps for Pillar One: Embrace

- How can you personalize each of the following for your journey?
    » Embrace the concept of impermanence.
    » Get comfortable with being uncomfortable.
    » Relax into the use of humor.
    » Acknowledge fear and overwhelm.
- Assess the level of openness in your relationship with your child. Where are you right now? Where are they? Where would you like to be?
- Try some of these conversation starters that feel right for you.
    » What do you need from us?
    » What about being out makes you most happy?
    » What about coming out makes you most scared or nervous?
- Check in with yourself and look ahead.
- Where are you right now? Record your goals.
    » One-week goal
    » One-month goal
    » One-year goal

. . . . .

This is not a race . . . there is no deadline. Be gentle with yourself and with your child. These are all small steps in understanding yourself better and building a strong relationship with your child. Take your time. And remember . . . you are not alone!

Pillar Two: Educate and Unlearn Bias

Welcome this opportunity to learn who your child is, understand what they are experiencing, and get clarity on the current climate for all LGBTQ+ people. Do you know your personal learning style or preference? Are you a visual, auditory, or interactive learner? Do you like reading books or listening to podcasts? Perhaps you prefer talking with others with lived experience or those who are experts on a topic?

My kids always joke that if I'm reading, the house better not catch fire because it would burn down around me. I completely lose myself in the magic of words and have always found great comfort in books, magazines, and online articles and blogs. (Although truth be told, I will always prefer a book; I think it is a sensory thing.) While the element of escape is part of the attraction, there is also the pursuit of understanding, whatever the topic may be. So, while this learning phase took place under extreme duress, a part of me thoroughly enjoyed every minute!

I know how daunting the prospect of doing a deep dive into research about the LGBTQ+ community is, but it is a worthy and even enjoyable endeavor. As you learn, comfort, power, understanding, and peace are possible. You will discover strategies for overcoming obstacles, coping techniques for overwhelm, and a plethora of stigma-busting information that can put your mind at ease.

Remember, growth is the ultimate goal.

An easy place to begin is to define the letters in the initialism LGBTQIA+. While I use LGBTQ for my podcast because that was most common when I started it in 2019, and I use LGBTQ+ throughout this book because it is most common now, I want to offer an even more complete definition since you will encounter it out in the world. Most people know *L* (lesbian), *G* (gay), *B* (bisexual), *T* (transgender). The letters, numbers (such as 2 for two-spirited), and symbols that follow are relatively recent additions that can be more confusing. While general consensus from organizations such as HRC and GLAAD define *Q* as queer, there are some that use it to refer to *questioning*. Visibility, understanding, and deepening bodies of research add intersex *I* to the list. (Fun fact: approximately 1.7 percent of the population is born intersex, which is close to the number of people born with red hair![1])

The A represents aromantic or asexual. These are similar but not the same. Aromantics experience little to no romantic attraction and asexual people experience little to no sexual attraction. The "+" represents all other orientations and identities.

In this pillar, we are going to take an in-depth look at the coming out process—for your child and for you—the different stages involved, what to be aware of, and where to find support. We are also going to discuss your support systems—what you currently have, what you need, and how to get it. Research information and options will be sprinkled throughout the pillar. The pillar will close with detailed information on mental health and substance use and abuse, how to recognize it, and how to find support.

CHAPTER FIVE

The Coming Out Process for Your Teen

Owning our story and loving ourselves through that
process is the bravest thing we'll ever do.

—BRENÉ BROWN

We knew soon after Connor came out that we needed guidance and significant education outside of individual therapy. We reached out to our local youth and family services agency, where we connected with Kate, a therapist and LGBTQ+ advocate and educator. From the moment Steve and I first met with Kate, we felt like a weight had been lifted. She met us where we were, which was frankly a bit frenetic. We were loaded with a billion questions, and she helped us begin to organize our thoughts and work through the layers of feelings. Kate's warmth and compassion put us at ease, and the comfort of her self-expression and appropriate sharing of her life experiences gave us confidence that she knew exactly what she was talking about. She has supported Steve and me separately, as we've had our own experiences within each of the transformations, and she has supported us as a couple.

The second most valuable thing Steve and I learned from Kate in those first few months after Connor came out was the coming out process. One of the best things about understanding the coming out process is having a glimpse into what our kids experience as they search for and express identity. It may seem drastic or dramatic, but it is part of the process for our teens as they try to figure out who they are and where they fit into this world.

If you are thinking, "Wait, there's a *process*??" The answer is yes, and it explains so much! Reading and learning about the stages of coming out blew me away. I was at once relieved, hopeful, and angry: relieved because understanding the stages answered so much of what Connor had experienced and was still experiencing; hopeful because we knew a little better how to support him and what resources to seek; angry because this information was not readily available. We had to jump through so many hoops and lose countless nights of sleep just to get to this point.

The coming out process or stages of coming out that I refer to are derived from the Cass Identity Model. It was originally created in 1979 by Vivienne Cass, who was the first to treat gay and lesbian identity development as normal developmental stages as opposed to a mental health problem.[1] Before those of you who have bisexual, transgender, or queer children get alarmed, know that in 1979 the terms used were "gay," "lesbian," and "identity." Much has shifted in the past forty-plus years; hundreds of studies, oodles of research, and vast opening of minds have occurred. Along with new understanding, more specific language has become accepted and preferred; I've updated the language to accurately reflect where we are now.

While language has evolved, most experts agree that Cass's model is still incredibly accurate for describing and understanding the coming out process. So take a moment to grab a notebook or your Post-it tabs because you will definitely use this section as a reference going forward.

Stage One: Identity and/or Orientation Confusion

In this initial phase, your child begins to realize they are different from their peers, causing a wide range of thoughts and emotions from shock to amazement to fear. In this stage, their thoughts, feelings, and attractions are beginning to surface consistently. As they contemplate that big question—who am I?—they will cycle through wanting to reject the thoughts and feelings, to denying the thoughts and feelings, to potentially accepting them.[2]

This stage is internal. You will likely have no idea it is happening, especially if your child feels any fear or shame mixed in. In real time, it can last months, even years.

Think about it: How many times will a thought or a feeling or an attraction come up and then be rejected—and then another, and it's rejected. That singular loop can go on for quite some time. That enormous question—who am I?—will likely spin in their minds as they consider the possibilities. They will reject and deny until they finally realize their personal truth.

Imagine what a personal hell that must be for our children. Layer on top of that the possible external factors and you have a recipe for self-loathing, isolation, shame, depression, anxiety, and anger. The subsequent behaviors based on these feelings will likely be our only clue that something is going on.

When Connor came out to us, he was a sophomore in high school. As he began sharing with us his journey up to that point, we learned that he began to realize he felt different from his friends in seventh grade. He went through every one of the above thoughts and feelings: rejecting the idea, being terrified of the idea, denying the mere thought of being gay, feeling so angry, loathing himself, and eventually isolating himself. He looped through these feelings over and over for three years. My heart still aches when I think about how alone he felt, how hard he worked to put up the everything-is-awesome facade, and how scared he was to tell us.

If you happen to realize what is going on with your child in this stage, the best thing you can do is provide support and let them know how much they are loved unconditionally. It will be hard, but it is vitally important that you wait for them to come out to you. Do not out them. This process is important.

Stage Two: Identity/Orientation Comparison

In stage two your child will start to wrap their head around the possibility that they are lesbian, gay, bisexual, transgender, queer, or any other sexual orientation or gender identity. Cass calls it *comparison* because your child is internally comparing themselves to all other ways of being in this world.[3] This is a process within a process, as this acknowledgment phase can expand and contract for a while. Just breathe.

In this stage, feelings of isolation and alienation are common. Your child will wonder if it is a phase and will begin to look externally for an explanation. Their curiosity and desire to learn about sexual orientation, gender identity, and LGBTQ+ resources will develop.

It is imperative to encourage them to talk about the loss of heterosexual life expectations and to allow them to grieve the change in *their* movie reel. I know I usually refer to our movie reel experience, but it is vitally important to recognize that our children have their own version, and they need to work through their feelings and thoughts around that to move forward.

Steve, Connor, and I had no clue about this stage until much further down the road. Connor had completely skipped it. I mean, really, what teen wants to explore and work through their feelings—especially the messy ones? Here is one of the significant problems skipping a stage causes, though: all those feelings of isolation, self-loathing, and grief get stuffed way down. And even though it may seem lovely if we could just ignore anything uncomfortable or painful and it would just go away, the reality is quite the opposite. The longer it stays in, the more sideways and messier it comes back out.

Connor felt he was finished with his coming out when he told us. At the time, none of us realized it was only the beginning. This is not at all uncommon. Many people think that verbally sharing this very personal information with a trusted person is the pinnacle of their journey, but it's just a beautiful landmark along the way.

Stage Three: Identity/Orientation Tolerance

In this stage, your child begins to realize that they are not the only one who is different. They may begin to look for an LGBTQ+ community or social group for support and a safe haven.[4] Connor did not have any interest in these groups when he was in high school because he was still dealing with intense internal judgment that he projected as others judging him. However, now that he has worked through so much and connected with his authentic self, he seeks LGBTQ+ friendships and social opportunities. Time, patience, and breathing yield progress.

According to Cass, in this stage, some may come to terms with parts of their identity and/or orientation but not completely embrace it, leading them to live a double life.[5] Self-loathing and shame are still very common in this stage, so be aware. Depending on the level of their struggle, it may be a good idea to add a professional therapist to the mix—specifically one who works with LGBTQ+ youth.

Remember, this is not a race. There is no deadline. Put in the time and work now. I promise it will pay off later!

It is okay to gently encourage your child to find a positive group where they feel safe and connected. One of my favorite online resources for teens is The Trevor Project's TrevorSpace. It is safe and moderated by trained professionals.

Today's technology makes it far too easy to slip into the dark underbelly of the internet. Knowing this allows you to be proactive and aware as you talk with your teen. If they don't find the right resources, they WILL find the wrong ones. I don't want to detour too much on this topic, so please understand this is very general and for educational purposes.

Just as there are those who prey on straight kids, there are those who prey on young LGBTQ+ kids on the internet, on apps, and out in the world. What may seem to be an innocent Google for information may lead down a dark path before your child is aware. I completely understand that these conversations can be uncomfortable, but I promise that it is better to have them before your child is caught up in what could be quite damaging.

Stage Four: Identity/Orientation Acceptance

In this stage, your child will begin to accept rather than just tolerate their identity and/or orientation. Cass notes that they become more open to forming friendships with other LGBTQ+ people, and most importantly, they realize they can have a happy, healthy, and fulfilling life.[6] In essence, they begin to breathe again and allow the feeling of "I will be okay."

At this point, they will begin coming out to those close to them.

One of the topics of debate around the coming out process is who gets to tell whom and when. Every family is different, so aside from the obvious advice—you know best who you need to tell and who your child should tell. I firmly believe this is your child's story, and they decide who gets to know and when. They also get to decide that they tell no one at all. It absolutely should be a conversation—or many conversations. Ask open-ended questions like "Who do you want to tell?" and "Can you help me understand why you do or don't want to tell people?" Their focus will likely be on their friends and family members. When it comes to telling your friends, that is more up to you, but allowing them to be part of the conversation is still a good idea.

One of the elements that really helps and makes this stage unique is being able to see themselves in others, whether in peers, the media, literature, or in the safety of in-person or virtual gatherings. When any person coming out (it doesn't matter how old they are) realizes they are not alone in this world, they shift from denial and all of the difficult emotions that go along with the early stages to allowing themselves the possibility of joy and connection. It's almost an audible sigh of relief as they realize they will be okay!

Stage Five: Identity/Orientation Pride

According to Cass, it is in this stage that your child will develop a sense of pride in their sexual orientation and/or gender identity and want to let people know who they are.[7] You will notice their confidence blossoming and a true embracing of self. It is quite a beautiful shift to be a part of and to observe!

Now, be warned that their social and political viewpoints may swing in this stage to be us vs. them, LGBTQ+ vs. straight, etc. Breathe through it. This is necessary for them to figure out what resonates with them. It may be the first time they have considered viewpoints outside of what they have learned at home or school. It has the potential to be messy, so know that ahead of time and adopt the choosing-your-battles approach. You know that the more you push back on something, the more your teen will gravitate to the polar opposite of what you are saying!

Remember, this is part of their process, part of learning about their community and broadening their viewpoints. As uncomfortable as this may be for you, remember this is their process, not yours. Encourage them to use their critical thinking skills. To ask questions. To be curious. To learn. You absolutely do not need to agree, but practice keeping that to yourself by silently repeating—this is a healthy part of their process. This is not forever. That being said, it is likely that as they continue to embrace who they are and figure out where and how they fit in this world, their views will differ from yours—and that is okay. That is a lovely reflection of the support and autonomy you have given them over time.

Your child may also experience anger in this stage regarding reactions from other people or the broader community, including national or world views of the LGBTQ+ community. This is okay too. We have been taught to tamp down and discourage anger when it is actually a valuable, informational tool. Like the exercise with fear, see it, validate it, and explore why it is showing up. Encourage your child to acknowledge and work through the anger with you or a trusted professional. In doing that, they can learn healthy coping mechanisms and tools to manage both their internal and external realities.

By learning what works best for them to handle others' reactions with grace and without defensiveness, they build a solid emotional and mental foundation for moving forward. While every person has their own unique way of showing up in the world, here are a couple of examples of how grace without defensiveness might look. The first is the classic: holding your head high and knowing when to walk away. If your child has a little more of an edge to them, they could come up with a one-liner that positively embodies who they are, sets a clear boundary, and returns the human element to the equation. "Who I am is not a choice, but being a bigot is," or "Just because you don't understand someone doesn't make their existence invalid," are examples of strong statements that can remind someone that LGBTQ+ teens are human too. Dehumanization and objectification are two common tactics by those who are anti-LGBTQ+ or who think they are anti-LGBTQ+. Engaging in a neutral or positive way makes it difficult for the other person to ignore your child's humanity. This takes lots of practice–for you and for them! Allow them the space to be in situations so they can learn. I know it is super hard, but resist the mama bear temptation to step in and protect!

Stage Six: Identity/Orientation Synthesis

In this final stage, Cass notes that your child will integrate their sexual orientation and/or gender identity with all other aspects of self. They realize that being gay, lesbian, bisexual, transgender, or queer is just one part of who they are—not their entire identity.[8] Like stage five, stage six is beautiful to observe. You can almost see the illumination with each light bulb moment. It's one of those moments where you just feel like shouting, "yay!" They are truly connecting with or appreciating who they are. They begin to be able to move fluidly through their life without defining spaces as gay or straight.

One afternoon the weekend of Connor's graduation from NYU, we sat at a little dive pizzeria in Brooklyn, and Connor shared with me that he finally felt settled in who he is. He finally realized that being gay is just one of the million beautiful pieces that make him uniquely him. I will hold that moment in my heart forever.

Coming out as LGBTQ+ does not just happen once. It is a lifelong process of discovering, accepting, and sharing one's sexual orientation and/or gender identity with others. Even if it is with expansions and contractions, working through these stages and steps builds emotional, physical, mental, and spiritual health. Most importantly, working through the process ends the pain of secrecy and isolation.

It is important to note that some people CHOOSE not to come out publicly or be specific about their orientation and/or identity for various reasons, including concerns for safety, religious barriers, being shunned by family and friends, potential discrimination at work or within healthcare, and simply because they feel it's their business. Understanding this very real and necessary reality for many allows space to hold that one's orientation and/or identity does not depend on them coming out.

Know that there is no one right way to go through this process. It is a uniquely individual process that may not be as overt as "I'm gay" and each of our kids will have their own experiences and feelings along the way. You may be uncomfortable with allowing this to be their process. Embrace the discomfort. Love and accept your child where they are at this moment in time! That is what they need and want most from us.

Ponder and Reflect

Grab your journal and reflect! Don't overthink it. Just let your thoughts and feelings flow onto the page.

- Journal notes and observations about your child's process. Make notes about where they struggle AND where you struggle. Next to each struggle, make a list of actions and/or support that would help.
- What personal work can you do so that you can show up for your child in the way you want to?
- What personal work can you do so that you can support your child if you feel they are comparing themselves with others?
- What are a few ways you can support your child throughout these stages?
- What are some ways that *you* need support during their coming out process?
- Do you need to unlearn any biases?
- What were two of your most important lessons you learned as you read about the coming out process?

. . . . .

Do your best to honor your child's wishes; remember, this is their story to tell.

CHAPTER SIX

The Coming Out Process for YOU

Knowledge is the antidote to fear.

—RALPH WALDO EMERSON

Yes, there is a process for YOU!

If this concept is new to you or you are thinking, "Um, I'm just here to learn how to support; I don't need a process," I ask that you humor me and just read this chapter for fun.

Whether you were surprised by your child's coming out or you had a feeling for years before they officially told you, there is still a process, and it is an important one to embrace so that you can create and nourish an authentic relationship with your child. As we focus on our child and their process, our other children and their joys and challenges, our spouses or partners and being present in that relationship, other family members, friends, work, and so on—we forget (or perhaps more accurately, have nothing left to give to) ourselves!

Enter a process created just for us—for parents, allies, family members, and friends. Like the coming out process for our child, we may go back and forth through these steps multiple times, but that is okay. Be gentle with yourself and ask your child to be patient with you too. Remember, seeing your humanity allows them space to be human, connect to their authentic self, and love themselves and others.

Years ago, when I was first researching this concept, I came across helpful guidance from Strong Family Alliance that gives seven stages in the journey for parents.[1] Over time and through experience, I added my own observations and nuggets of wisdom and created the following six stages for parents.

Stage One: Shock

This stage applies only if you had absolutely no idea, like us. The initial shock typically lasts only a few days but, of course, can vary. It is a natural reaction. There is no shame in it. Allow yourself the time and space to process through it and settle into the news.

You may ask questions or make statements you wouldn't usually ask or make, such as "Are you sure?" Yep, we did that. Ugh. I am sick every time I think back to that. Thankfully, we've discussed it many times since and apologized for asking what we now know is a pretty insensitive question. Thankfully, Connor is way past it and completely understands where we were at that point.

I share all of this with you for two reasons: 1. You are human and will mess up—own it, apologize, and move forward; and 2. I want you to understand that your child coming out to you is something they likely thought about for weeks, months, or even years before they said it aloud to you. **They. Are. Sure.**

Stage Two: Denial

Not everyone experiences this stage, but it is essential to understand as you will likely have someone in your life who will. As we know, it is always easier to take something in stride if we understand it.

Here are a few reactions that are a sign of denial to be aware of:

- **Hostility (general and toward your child):** feeling extreme or prolonged anger about the news, telling your child, "no child of mine will be queer," or using other hurtful language.

- **Avoidance:** not acknowledging the information being shared, changing the subject when it is brought up, or looking for reasons or excuses to avoid the topic.
- **Indifference:** different from avoidance in that your child's sexual orientation and/or gender identity is acknowledged, but only to convey the message "if you choose that lifestyle, I don't want to hear about it."
- **Rejection:** any form of rejecting the news, the idea, the person—or all of the above. It can also be the common fallback of thinking *it's just a phase or a form of rebellion.*

If this stage seems to linger for you or whomever you are observing it in, seek guidance. This is imperative. Denial must be faced and worked through to be able to move forward.

Stage Three: Guilt

This is a tough one and can be particularly messy.
Here are the signs:

- You may feel like you've done something wrong.
- You view your child's coming out as a problem. You may question, "what causes it?"
- You may spend endless hours asking yourself if you were a bad parent or wondering what you did that you made your child "different."

In seeking an answer here, you will almost always land on yourself as the one to blame. I want you to read this very carefully:

There is NO ONE to blame. This is NOT a CHOICE. Your child's sexual orientation and/or gender identity is just one piece of who they are.

Finally, shame may be wrapped with guilt, making it difficult for you to share these feelings with anyone.

If this is striking a chord with you, I want you to stop and take that calming breath. I like to use box breathing to calm myself, but 4-7-8 breathing also works great! (Inhale for four counts, hold for seven counts, exhale for eight counts). Once you feel centered again, please read and consider the following three points very carefully.

First, please understand that these feelings are a normal part of the process. It is always easiest to blame ourselves or to feel like we have failed in some way. If you are susceptible to this, now is the time to be aware that this is a coping mechanism, albeit a maladaptive one, and I want you to move through it. Acknowledge your feelings, as uncomfortable as they are, and keep moving forward.

Second, stop looking for something you've done wrong and blaming yourself. Stop with the "if only I had done (fill in the blank) better" self-shaming. This isn't about anything you have done or not done. This is who your child is. Being lesbian, gay, bisexual, transgender, or queer isn't a result of environment, trauma, or any other "happening" any more than being straight. Just as there are many shades and phases of night and day, dawn and dusk, midday and midnight, so are there many possibilities of sexual orientation and gender identity.

Third, if you work through the steps above, as well as the reflection work at the end of each chapter and still find yourself stuck in the shame spiral, please seek professional guidance.

Stage Four: Feelings Expressed

During this stage, we begin to work through the full gamut of emotions. We can only reach this stage if denial, guilt, and shame have been acknowledged and we are working through them.

While the movie reel analogy can happen at any stage, it usually occurs here. In this stage, emotions will spill out of you regardless of time, place, or provocation. What comes out may shock you, but breathe through it and ride the waves. This is a necessary step. Holding emotion in will only cause it to come out sideways later.

Steve experienced this in a big way. He was always one who could ride the waves of emotion and life in general and never felt any need or desire for therapy. However, he realized that he had just been stockpiling all of the big emotions—the worry, the unknown, the fear—when he absolutely lost his mind on an employee. He began seeing a therapist on a monthly basis after that, and that little extra support has made an enormous difference.

Even though I am a naturally expressive and emotional person, this stage took me by surprise. As I learned to breathe through it and just let the emotions come and go, I realized that I was simultaneously working through and letting go of decades of pain and unexpressed emotions. Talk about messy! I cried in front of our middle school principal, a Starbucks barista, my dry cleaner, my doctor, and, probably most importantly, I cried in front of our kids. I had always been cautious to guard them from what I considered to be an over-expression of my feelings or my sadness. This was the beginning of one of many new chapters of allowing my children to see my humanness. This is where communication will open and where healing may begin, thus allowing for more profound, transparent, and authentic relationships and experiences.

If this stage of the process brings up negative or difficult emotions for you, please, please, please do not share those feelings with your child. You absolutely are entitled to and need to process these feelings, but they are not your child's responsibility. They have their own process. Work through them with your spouse, partner, friend, or professional.

Stage Five: Decision Making and Authentic Awareness

In this stage you are ready to understand where everyone is in their individual process. After you work through the emotional outbursts, trauma, mourning, freaking out, or otherwise expressing anger, hurt, fear, and any other negativity and emotions, you will have the mental clarity to decide how you would like to proceed. Proceeding requires you to be aware of where you are right now in your process. There are a few options.

One option is to be an all-in, present, and supportive parent. This choice is best if the air has been cleared and you feel your relationship has been repaired and is at a place of mutual trust and honesty. Here you can focus not only on your child who is out but on your other children as well.

However, if you feel fragile or unable to process anymore at this point, then let your child know that you need some time and work through it with a professional or a trusted friend. It is okay if you are here. The most important things to focus on are being open and honest, being gentle, and giving yourself space.

Finally, if there is still tension or arguments or unsettled issues, which is a continuation of stage four, take some time to consider why. Is it fear, and if so, fear of what? Is it religious belief? Political stance? The unknown? I know this is hard to do, and I'm asking you to be extremely vulnerable. If you are in this place, know there is no judgment. You must walk through the discomfort to heal and move forward.

Keep in mind that if your unresolved concerns lead to arguments with your LGBTQ+ child, locking horns will get you nowhere fast. Instead, look for personal support. Try attending a parents' meeting like PFLAG, having coffee with another parent with an LGBTQ+ child, listening to a podcast, or meeting with a professional who specializes in supporting families with LGBTQ+ members. You may learn something that will guide you in a better way.

Stage Six: True Acceptance

This stage may be the most significant shift of all. The shift from loving your teen with exceptions to loving your teen unconditionally will transform your relationship with them forever. Celebrate the beauty of their uniqueness and know to the depth of your soul they are exactly who they are meant to be in this world.

In this stage, you may also experience the following:

- Working through your guilt
- Reflecting on and creating a new stance on gay jokes and other sensitive language

- Beginning to understand and be aware of problems you unknowingly created for your child
- Advocating for your child and the greater LGBTQ+ community
- Beginning to help educate others

This is a stage of HUGE growth opportunities. Allow yourself to be open. Getting to this stage takes conscious effort and work, but it is beyond worth it! I look at Connor and want to burst with love and pride as I see his courage, perseverance, and witty personality. Of course, there are still struggles—that is part of life. When you see your child getting back up when they've been knocked down (or when they've knocked themself down!), and they continue to figure out who they are, we just need to be there for them. Your most important job is to love unconditionally, support, and encourage your child. They must know wherever they are physically or mentally, they are not alone.

For those of you who have other kids, know and be aware that they will have their own processes to work through. Because my three younger kids, Isabelle, Grace, and Rowan, were thirteen, eleven, and nine when Connor first came out and went through some of the scariest parts of his journey, it was a juggling act just to decide what was okay to share with who and when. It required a ton of discretion, education, and gentleness. All six of us have had our own processes, and your family members will all have their own processes. I find it extraordinary how flexible, curious, and full of unconditional love kids really are. My children (and young humans in general) have amazed me time and time again with the depth of their empathy and compassion, their ability to critically think and problem solve, and their capacity to love unconditionally.

Now, please don't think for a moment that I am trying to paint some rosy picture of perfection—far from it! Each family will go through a process of revealing cracks and imperfections—of messing up and allowing each other to have ugly days. Though it may be messy, having patience with and honoring this process will allow you to grow closer as a family. Removing the pressure of some unattainable expectation of perfection makes all the difference. One of Connor's tattoos says "Settle into the Chaos," and I love it because it is a reminder of this valuable shift that we all made.

I created my own version of this shift and state of mind:

Embrace the beauty in the messiness!

You may find that your family will ride the ebbs and flows of the tide. Every family and every child within will create their unique way of balancing and swaying with the movement. Just like you can't control the ocean, don't try to direct your family's tide. Take that deep breath and let go.

Don't rush through the work—remember two things: this isn't a competition, and there is no deadline! Use either of these as your mantra and put it on repeat in your head.

Ponder and Reflect

Grab your journal and reflect! Don't overthink it. Just let your thoughts and feelings flow onto the page.

In each stage, note your struggles and your victories in your journal. What support or information would be helpful?

- Stage One: Shock
- Stage Two: Denial
- Stage Three: Guilt
- Stage Four: Feelings Expressed
- Stage Five: Decision Making and Authentic Awareness
- Stage Six: True Acceptance
    » Did any of these stages feel surprising or uncomfortable? If so, why?

CHAPTER SEVEN

Support, Support, Support Part One

We don't have to do it all alone.
We were never meant to.

—BRENÉ BROWN

*H*umans tend to celebrate with many but suffer alone. We aren't meant to, though. Struggles, crises . . . heck, sometimes even your child's math homework, call for outside support.

Support can come in many forms, sometimes in ways we didn't know existed before we started to look. Support falls under education because I think it is essential to erase the misinformation and stigmas surrounding different types of support.

Support has many components to it. We're going to look at the components of faith and spirituality, family, friends, support groups, and therapy. There may be other areas that add to your support system, and that is great. What does your support system look like right now? Remember, there is no right or wrong answer. Do you lean on your faith or spirituality practice? Family? Friends? A therapist or other professional support system?

Wherever you are right now, it's okay. As you read the following two chapters, I want you to think about what you need, what your child needs, and what your family needs. Take note of which ideas feel good and which put you on edge. Part of this process is pure awareness: allowing yourself to notice and feel and then taking appropriate action.

Faith and Spirituality

Faith and spirituality are first on the list because not only do many of us keep them in our support toolbox but also because I know you may have felt worried or scared when your child came out as LGBTQ+ because of what you have been taught.

I grew up in a Christian home, so that is the lens through which I have experienced much of my life. I recognize that while many faiths share similar views to Christianity, many others do not. Part of this section will address Christianity specifically, and the other part will look at belief systems in general.

I believe that a person's faith and belief system is personal, precious, and worthy of respect from others.

I have made a significant discernment over the past few years. Religion encompasses the institution itself, meaning the generations of humans who have translated, created rules, and otherwise influenced what is widely seen as "right and wrong," "good and bad," "evil and holy," etc.

Faith and spirituality are that very personal relationship you have with your higher power and knowing that an entity greater than you has your back. This was a massive shift for me because I lived decades of my life in fear of doing or saying the wrong thing and even thinking that I was damned no matter what. My shift from fear of damnation and the dogmas of religion to feeling loved and supported by a higher power has freed my soul to have an authentic spiritual relationship for the first time in my life!

Religion or faith is a natural go-to source of support for some people, and one that may suddenly become complicated and fraught with worry and fear because of what many religions teach about the LGBTQ+ community.

I remember thinking, "Is Connor damned?" when he first came out. My childhood teaching said, "Yes." Terror held me in such a tight grip that I thought I might shatter. And then I finally remembered to breathe, just enough to be able to hear my intuition saying, "He's not; learn more. There is information out there; just keep looking."

And so I did. This was when Steve and I met Kate, the therapist, LGBTQ+ advocate, and educator I mentioned a few chapters back. In one of our first meetings with her, I remember being twisted in knots of fear and overwhelm and needing answers . . . lots of them! I vividly recall my inarticulate gush of feelings, questions, and urgency, finally reaching my root question: Is Connor going to hell?

Kate handed me Susan Cottrell's book *Mom, I'm Gay*, and my life changed forever. I don't say that lightly or for dramatic effect—this book opened my eyes and spoke to me in a way that allowed me to begin the shift into my authentic self and find my true spiritual path.

As I began my spiritual work and allowed my mind and spirit to stretch and grow, I began to feel hope. I saw that the labels, the condemnation, and the rules were just a facade of misinformation, ignorance, and FEAR. This was when I began to see faith as love and a relationship with a higher power. (Higher power can be God, the universe, angels, love . . . whatever resonates with you.) Tuning into that little voice has turned my faith and spiritual life upside down.

It is okay to take the time you need. Your discoveries may feel uncomfortable at times, but your result could be a beautiful and authentic discovery of a faith that lights you up inside. Like I said at the beginning of the chapter, I believe faith encompasses all belief systems. Do this work around what resonates with you.

Have patience with your child's faith journey if they have one or if that is a family value. When Connor first came out, I was devastated whenever he would express anger toward God or not want to go to church with us. As I allowed myself to breathe a bit and allowed Connor space, I was able to see it from his point of view. For the few years leading up to his coming out until quite recently, he was angry with God for creating him as he first thought, different, and later accepted, gay.

And who can blame him, right? There is nothing easy about being a gay teenager. Not one thing.

Allow your child to detox and work their way through the coming out process; whether they find faith again is part of their journey. If they find faith or spirituality, it may look different than yours, and it may look different than it did when they were a child, but that's okay. The important thing is to allow them their journey.

I believe that religion can get in the way of faith. What I mean by that is the institution, the rules, the dogma, and the human-influenced prejudices. The moment I truly wrapped my head around this concept was the moment that love, rather than fear, began to influence my faith.

The shift to unconditional love and peace takes time, and I am still working on it. I'm sharing this with you because I don't want you to give up. While everyone's faith and spirituality look different, if faith is important to you, the strength and support you receive from leaning on it are incomparable.

Family

Okay, phew! Moving on to family.

Family can be complicated. They can be a source of incredible support, intense anxiety, indescribable pain, or all three, depending on the day and the family member. There can be moments of beauty and love—and then moments of "Wow, people really do think and believe this way, and I'm related to them!"

Based on conversations I've had with parents and allies over the past few years, it seems that most of us have some combination of the above.

As I consider the ways I have shifted, opened my mind and heart, and embraced the *me* who was buried so deep inside, I realize that the gift of clarity and discernment ranks right up there in the genuinely remarkable outcomes!

Consider how you've grown in awareness and appreciation for the little signs of love and support from family members. Of course, the obvious "we love your child and support them no matter what" statements are the best, but this is not necessarily the way everyone expresses themself. So, recognizing the small signs—the smiles, hugs, stories shared, genuine interest—these are the little pieces of support that can lift us up and remind us that we are loved, that our child is loved, and that at least one family member has our back.

Think about the little signs, the affirmations you or your child have received from family members. Celebrate those! Honor that everyone has a process as well. So many people, parents and kids alike, have shared frustration at family members who don't say the right things at first, or who remain in the shock stage for a while. This frustration is a perfect example of using AND. You can be frustrated AND you can allow these family members time. Sometimes people need a little extra processing, even internal reconciliation, to reach affirmation.

Over time and through the sharing of so many stories from others, I have compiled guidelines and boundaries for interacting with family. Let's start with four guidelines for family relationships; as you understand the guidelines, you'll be ready to set healthy boundaries for you and your family. Use the following two questions to identify which of these guidelines may be helpful for you.

1.   Does this apply to any of my family members?
2.   How can I adapt this guideline to work best for me?

YES, WE ALL NEED GUIDELINES FOR FAMILY RELATIONSHIPS!

My family of origin and extended family has always been a bit complicated. I'm guessing many of you can identify with that. Think about the many intersecting pieces that informed your formative years: where you lived, your race, your religion, your family's access to education and income, and so on. Now consider the natural growth that occurs as you age, as well as any intentional personal work that you may have done, and add that to the equation. These factors can cause family dynamics to shift. Sometimes those shifts are smooth, and sometimes they encourage healthy boundaries and positive reframing to maintain relationships.

ACKNOWLEDGE AND TAKE RESPONSIBILITY FOR YOUR SHIFTS

This is the first guideline. Acknowledge and take responsibility for your shifts as you navigate what boundaries look like in your family. When you can embrace who you are, the work you have done or are doing, and stay connected to self, then healthy boundaries are far easier to set. I've spent almost eight years working through emotional trauma, shifting my mindset, educating myself, and discovering who I truly am. I recognize that I am the one who has changed. I have embraced the fact that I have value and purpose.

In one family I worked with, one side of the family was fully affirming and eager to learn and support their LGBTQ+ family member. In contrast, the other side of their family had members who ranged from apathetic to strongly anti-LGBTQ+. The first few months were a roller coaster of emotions and wishes, as in "I wish my extended family would change." Once this family shifted their focus from looking outward to looking at their nuclear family dynamic, as well as their individual internal dynamics, they were able to begin identifying what was really important to them. In doing this, they were able to achieve clarity around and own the shifts they were making. As each did their personal work and implemented healthy shifts in their lives that ranged from meditation and personal care (sleep and exercise) to entrenching themselves in LGBTQ+ education, their awareness increased, as did their responsibility for each small shift along the way.

MAKE THE NEEDS OF YOUR NUCLEAR FAMILY YOUR NUMBER ONE PRIORITY

This next guideline focuses on your priorities. On the morning of Connor's high school graduation party, a little over two years after he came out, my brother decided that was the perfect moment to lecture my kids on the "choice" of being gay as well his misguided thoughts on why there should be straight pride parades. You know how you have those pivotal life moments that retain their clarity no matter how much time passes? This was one of those moments for me. I stopped the conversation and told my brother that sharing his intolerance was not okay and not allowed in my home.

All mothers have a mama bear hibernating inside. And all parents have unique triggers that awaken that protective instinct. I don't think it's assumptive to believe that having your child verbally attacked is one of those triggers! So, this second guideline is a no-brainer: make the needs of your immediate family your sacred priority. Period.

EXAMINE YOUR CORE BELIEFS

The next important guideline is to look at your core beliefs. One of the gifts of this journey is the gift of clarity. In a letter I received a few months after that graduation party conversation, my brother asked why my core beliefs had changed. So, I took time to deeply examine my core beliefs, and while this is an excerpt from the whole of my beliefs, I came to be certain of the following:

- I believe in love that is unconditional.
- I believe in kindness and that it is one of the most important traits we can teach our children and certainly one of the most important gifts we can give one another.
- I believe that family embodies unconditional love by supporting one another, offering guidance, encouraging each other to be authentic and loyal, and celebrating each person's uniqueness and talents.
- I believe that humor is essential to surviving life's ups and downs, and true joy is a by-product of that.

What I realized is that my core beliefs hadn't changed at all. What had changed was my adherence to the family playbook and adoption of a false belief that *their* core beliefs were also mine. This exercise allowed me to make this realization and fully connect with the real me. As heartbreaking as the entire ordeal was, it was the first time I wasn't afraid to set healthy boundaries. It allowed me much-needed introspection and a deeper understanding.

Clarifying, articulating, and embracing our core values makes decision making and boundary setting much easier. I encourage you to take the time to examine your core values. If they have always lived in your subconscious, like mine did, get them out of your head and onto paper.

Free write about them, meaning write whatever comes to mind; don't overthink. Notice what comes up for you. Walk away from the exercise and breathe. Come back with fresh eyes. Ask questions like:

- Is this value mine, or did I inherit it?
- Does this value feel aligned with who I am?
- How do I want to feel?
- Does this value support who I want to be in this world?

This exercise could take weeks or months to complete, and that is okay.

LET GO

Now it's time to truly let go! This is our last family guideline. There may come a time when you realize that members of your family do not have the ability or the desire to embrace, accept, affirm, or otherwise love unconditionally. I know how devastating and heartbreaking this can be. If you are anywhere along this path of realization, know that you are not alone! It is hard. It is painful. And you will get through it.

Journaling can be an incredible outlet during this time of letting go. Filling pages with your feelings is healing and therapeutic. You can also write letters that you never intend to send. This exercise is particularly helpful because when you have a specific person you are writing to, you can be much more precise in expressing your thoughts and feelings. Perhaps even more important, you can purge every bit of the good, bad, and ugly from your heart and then tear that letter up or light it on fire! This exercise purifies your heart and soul—and is so effective for letting go. It is also helpful to look to what comes next and list all of the possible ways forward. There will likely be tears, heartache, and sadness. These are all part of mourning a change in or even the end of a relationship.

Your process and the specifics of your heartache are unique. Think about what is weighing on your heart, mind, and soul. Do you need to let go of a wish or hope pertaining to someone else's actions? Or is your letting go process one of releasing internal heaviness?

Understand that the act of letting go is very personal and wide-ranging. Think of it as shedding something (or someone) that no longer serves a positive or healthy purpose in your life. It can be a burden, an expectation, a past trauma or wound, or a relationship.

Once you better understand your shifts, priorities, and beliefs and are ready to truly let go, you are prepared to embark upon the process of setting healthy boundaries.

SET BOUNDARIES

One more helpful word on family: BOUNDARIES. Learn how to set healthy boundaries. In my early forties, I was chatting with a friend on the phone and she very directly said, "Heather, you need to set boundaries." And my response was, "What are these boundaries you speak of?" I am here to tell you that you are never too young or too old to learn how to set healthy boundaries, as well as how to respect them. The value of boundaries is essential for us to practice and teach to our kids; the earlier, the better!

WHAT IS A BOUNDARY?

My favorite resource on this topic is the work completed by The University of Illinois Chicago. A healthy boundary is a line that clearly communicates what behaviors are acceptable to you. This boundary can be physical, emotional, or abstract, such as the value of your time and the space around you.[1]

WHY SET HEALTHY BOUNDARIES?

First and foremost, boundaries are a vital form of self-care. They also communicate how you wish to be treated by others, as well as your needs and wants. When you learn how to do this effectively, it allows you to show up authentically. Boundaries naturally beget respect.

HOW DO YOU SET HEALTHY BOUNDARIES?

Setting healthy boundaries begins within. Recognize that you are worthy of respect. Acknowledge any boundaries that may already be in place in your different relationships. Are they working to create positive relationships? Think about your needs and wants. Do existing boundaries need to be shifted or new ones created? Know that you will have different boundaries for different relationships. The way you communicate boundaries with each person will also be different. With one person, it may only take a few words. With another, it may be a long conversation. And with another, the boundaries may need to be written.

As your relationships shift over time, so will the boundaries you create.

Family can be challenging and complicated. It can also be supportive and comforting. It is common to feel isolated and sad on this journey, especially when it comes to complex relationships. Please remember that you are not alone. And you have choices.

Acclaimed author Billy Chapata said, "Understand that some people are only able to handle older versions of you. They will turn away from who you currently are because they don't know what growth looks like. You are not required to reprise older roles you once assumed in order to make other people comfortable." BRAVO!!! As humans, we are either growing, evolving, and living—or stuck in fear and dying. I choose the former. How about you?

Ponder and Reflect

Grab your journal and reflect! Don't overthink it. Just let your thoughts and feelings flow onto the page.

- Think about what faith or spirituality means to you.
- Write about how you envision spirituality will play a role in your life going forward.
- Lean into and onto your faith for support.

There will be more to come in the fourth pillar. For the sake of this exercise, though, remember it is important that boundaries are set verbally and written down.

- Yep, physically use paper and pen to work out any boundaries you feel are needed.
- Ask yourself what you need from your immediate and extended family, and communicate boundaries if necessary.

CHAPTER EIGHT

Support. Support. Support Part Two

Everyone needs a support system, be it family, friends, coworkers, therapists, or religious leaders. We cannot do life alone and expect to keep mentally, emotionally, and spiritually healthy. Everyone needs some sort of support system on which to rely.

—RICHELLE E. GOODRICH

In the last chapter, we covered the intimate support of spirituality and family. In support part two, we'll broaden our circle to include friendships and additional support through therapy and support groups. As you read, consider all the places you seek and find support and those where you wish you could find more support. This practice will help bring you clarity on what you need.

Friendships

Everyone needs at least one true blue, judgment-free, love-you-no-matter-what friend—the kind you can laugh, cry, and be silly with—the kind who can see you at your best and celebrate with you and see you at your worst and love you anyway.

My thoughts on friends are pretty simple. Cherish and nurture real friendships. If you find that you are lacking or wanting, cultivate new ones. And, perhaps most importantly, cut toxic relationships out of your life. Friends are the chosen family we make along the way. These same tenants work to help your kids navigate friendships. As you think about your friendships, think about how you can share this knowledge with your kids.

If you're thinking, "Heather, it's not that simple! How do I know who is true and who is toxic? How or where do I make new friends?"— here are some answers.

Right now, you are focusing on your relationship with your child. You are learning how to shift mentally, how to set boundaries, and how to delve into educating yourself on the LGBTQ+ community. Your priority is your child, yourself, and your immediate family unit. Real friends will support you, love you, and hold space for you. Toxic relationships will drag you down. You DO NOT need that kind of energy in your life.

I know that cultivating new friendships can be difficult, perhaps even scary or daunting. Probably the easiest way for adults to meet new people is through their work, faith community, kids' activities, and school community. It may be out of your comfort zone, but remember that it is in these moments of vulnerability that genuine connections are formed.

As an extroverted introvert, I am quite careful and guarded about who I allow in. I am truly blessed to have incredible friends in my life, with friendships that have been cultivated over many years. Even so, it took time to let each one in. I learned to be vulnerable; it was very messy, but it gave me the gift of being open to genuine support and love and the blessing of friendships where this love and support flows both ways. I have lost count of the times these ladies stepped in to help, whether it was driving my kids where they needed to be, bringing food when they knew I just didn't have it in me to cook, or holding my hand when I needed to cry, and I am beyond grateful.

Therapy

I believe everyone should see a therapist. I have seen the benefits in so many people's lives—inside AND outside of my family and myself—that I know beyond a doubt that it works.

Some of you may have grown up with negative messaging about therapy as I did, so considering it may feel very uncomfortable. Some avoid therapy because they have deeply held beliefs that therapy is a sign of weakness or an indicator that something is wrong with them. Others may feel therapy is a waste of time.

Though I had reservations, well before Connor came out, I started noticing little signs that seeing a therapist would be a good idea—a passage in a book would resonate, or I'd stumble upon positive research from a respected author, or someone would share a story about therapy being good support. Hmmm. Sit with the discomfort. I'm not telling you that you MUST do it; I'm asking you to allow yourself the time to consider it.

In the spring of 2015, a friend invited me to a self-care workshop. At that point in my life, I had zero understanding of boundaries and was incapable of saying "no." Guilt and "should" were my constant companions. I remember being intrigued by the idea of self-care, but truth be told, I had no idea what it actually meant. I recall sitting in the cozy, light-filled family room of the woman presenting the workshop and thinking, *"I'm allowed to take care of me?"*

It had never occurred to me that if I took care of myself, I could better care for everyone around me, let alone create my own extraordinary life! I remember feeling a blend of awe and anger: awe because I realized for the first time that I truly mattered, and anger because why on earth did I not know this before?!

The woman leading this workshop became my therapist, and I have been working with her ever since. For the first time, outside of Steve, I felt seen, I felt heard, and I felt understood. Over time, and with A LOT of work, I have found freedom. I've embraced my voice and my passion. I've discovered my strength and my confidence. I've transformed.

What YOU are experiencing right now is a transformation, an opportunity to grow and evolve. I know that right now, life may be challenging. Your child may be struggling. You may be struggling. If you have other children, they may be struggling. Your relationship with your spouse or partner may be struggling.

So, you have a choice: seek therapy (or professional support of some kind) or struggle through without that support. If you choose to find a therapist who resonates with your needs, you can have an objective person to whom you can say anything—ANYTHING—and receive feedback and advice that is holistic, researched, unbiased, and non-judgmental. Your well-being is their one and only priority. Depending on the modality your therapist practices (CBT, DBT, mindfulness, etc.), you will also learn tools and strategies for personal growth.

The friend who brought me to the self-care workshop told me that seeing a therapist makes her a better friend, wife, and mother because she gets all the stuff out that her husband and kids don't need to hear her ruminate on or process. That has always stayed with me because it's true! Think about it—at the very least, how good would it feel to be able to just get everything off your chest and out of your head? You may have a whole mess of feelings, both positive and negative, swirling around the idea of therapy. You won't know if it works for you until you try!

Now . . . the caveat is that finding a therapist who is right for you is a bit like dating, so be patient with the process and don't feel bad if you don't click with the first person you meet. You will know when you've met the right therapist for you. To get started, analyze the different areas of your life. The following questions will help you hone in on or prioritize the type of support you need:

- How well do you and your spouse communicate? [marriage therapy]
- Do you need a place outside of your home to vent or process? [private or group therapy]
- Do you need or would you benefit from guidance and support? [private therapy]

- Do you want guidance and support for the entire family? [family therapy]
- Do you have grief, trauma, or maladaptive coping mechanisms that you need to work through? [private trauma or grief-specific therapy]

Having a basic idea of what type of support you would most benefit from will help in the search.

It will come as no surprise that your LGBTQ+ child can be supported through therapy also. When I searched for a therapist to work with Connor, the process was more intensive. Since Connor was the one who needed a good match, he offered two requests: a therapist who was a gay man and one who would hold him accountable and call him on his BS with compassion. I pre-screened multiple therapists, and he met with my top five to ensure he found the right one. Steve and I wholeheartedly supported his needs, and we were grateful when, after a little trial and error, he found the right therapist for him.

After a little over a year working with his therapist, Connor headed off for his first year at NYU. It was a bit bumpy, especially with the interruption of the COVID pandemic, but it was an overall success in that the year included massive personal growth. One of the most significant factors? A therapist who fully understood every facet of him and whom he trusted.

I share all of this with you because I want you to be okay with the process and the work behind the transformation. The process of therapy looks different for everyone. There are different modalities and styles. Some therapists focus on behavior, while others focus on development or desired outcomes. In a general sense, there are four phases of the therapeutic process. The first is *orientation*. This is the getting-to-know-you phase. It will take time to build trust and a comfort level with your therapist. The second phase is *identification*. This one is self-explanatory. During this time, you and your therapist will clarify what you want and need to work on. The third phase is *exploration*. This is where you peel back the layers and do the work, both internal and external. Transformation occurs here. The fourth phase is *resolution*. At this time, you realize you have accomplished all you can with this therapist or that you need a break. Either way, give yourself a high five for the progress you've made.

Parent coaches, specifically ones who work with parents of LGBTQ+ kids, are another great option for support, especially if you are having difficulty finding a licensed therapist or are resistant to that step in any way. Available virtually and in person, they can work with you one-on-one, as a family, or within a group setting. One of the many benefits of working with a coach is that they typically have life experience, meaning they have been where you are, so they hold your experiences and provide support with wisdom and compassion that cannot be learned from a book.

As you seek this type of support, let go of the expectation for instant results. Not only is that unrealistic, but it will also leave you frustrated and lacking clarity. Each child has their own process. You have your own process, as does your spouse/partner. Allow the process to unfold. Breathe.

Community and Support Groups

Support groups are a great place to meet like-minded people who are on a similar journey. If you want the kind of community that will support and nurture you as you walk down this path, support groups are a great option. Facebook has a plethora of virtual support groups. PFLAG (formerly known as Parents, Families, and Friends of Lesbians and Gays) has monthly in-person meetings in many cities across the US and Canada and has affiliated groups internationally. Outright International, IGLYO, and Rainbow Railroad are fantastic international support and resource groups. Check out your local youth and family centers or mental health support organizations for support that ranges from one-on-one to group to experiential.

As we focus on our teens, other children, partners, and other family members, it's easy to forget to take time for ourselves to process everything coming at us. Seeking support—in whatever form—allows us to show up as the best version of ourselves. Thankfully, there are many types of support—some obvious and others we may take for granted. The end goal is that you feel supported and receive the guidance you seek and need.

I encourage you to share these options for support with your LGBTQ+ child, your other children, and your partner. There are so many LGBTQ+-specific support options available (see the reference section, as well as my website for a comprehensive list). If this time has brought tension into your home, or if you feel your children have questions and feelings that you are struggling to answer, consider seeing a family therapist. My website (chrysalismama.com) has recommendations and links to help you find the right therapist for you, your child, your marriage, and your family.

Ponder and Reflect

Grab your journal and reflect! Don't overthink it. Just let your thoughts and feelings flow onto the page.

- Think of one friend who has your back no matter what and vice versa.
- What would you like to tell them right now?
- Write a list of three traits that are important for a therapist to have.
- Write a list of three topics you would like to discuss with a therapist or share in a support group.

CHAPTER NINE

Understand Mental Health and Self-Harm

Hardships often prepare ordinary people for an extraordinary destiny.

—C. S. LEWIS

He was disappearing before our eyes, tortured and filled with self-loathing. While maintaining good grades at school, he was spiraling out of control and into a dark and dangerous place. Self-harm, substance use, and risky behaviors were his maladaptive coping mechanisms to ease the pain and intensity of his inner struggle. Terrified and wrought with worry, we naively thought we could love and support him enough to rescue him from his desperate hell. Thankfully, we quickly realized that we needed professional therapeutic guidance.[1]

This is an excerpt from an article I wrote for *Better Magazine* in 2018. It is still the best way to describe what Connor was experiencing as a seventeen-year-old. It is a description many families of LGBTQ+ teens likely can empathize with.

Mental Health

I am a huge proponent of mental health awareness and education. While I am delighted that mental health is no longer the overshadowed, ugly duckling of Western medicine and that encouragement to care for our mental health is almost on par with caring for our physical health, our country is in a mental health crisis, especially considering the toll the pandemic has taken.

According to *Mental Health America*'s annual State of Mental Health report, 11.5 percent of youth are experiencing severe major depression despite an increase in awareness.[2] The 2023 U.S. National Survey on the Mental Health of LGBTQ+ Young People, conducted by The Trevor Project, shares that rates of suicidal ideation and self-harm are highest among our eleven- to seventeen-year-olds, with 41 percent of LGBTQ+ young people seriously considering attempting suicide in the past year.[3] Adolescence is a critical period for mental health because many mental health disorders show onset during and directly following this developmental period. Nearly one in three teens ages thirteen to eighteen has an anxiety disorder, and that number continues to climb.[4]

These are startling numbers, and they beg for answers to some unsettling questions. First, why are the numbers still increasing when overall awareness is also increasing? Second, what are the underlying potential causes that all youth have in common? Third, what shifts are needed across the board (mental health professionals, parents/families, schools/organizations, and youth)?

Mental health is quite a large umbrella, so here is a fundamental breakdown of teen-specific signs and symptoms of depression and anxiety disorders:

DEPRESSION

- sadness
- feeling negative and worthless
- increased fatigue and sleep problems
- anxiety
- irritability and anger

- changes in appetite and weight
- poor performance in school
- school refusal
- feeling misunderstood and extremely sensitive
- substance abuse
- loss of interest in normal activities or social interaction
- self-harm
- suicide, including ideation and attempt

ANXIETY

- irritability
- restlessness
- difficulty concentrating
- avoiding normal activities or social interaction
- isolating from friends
- frequent headaches
- gastrointestinal issues
- fatigue
- sleep problems
- poor performance in school
- symptoms of panic attacks (rapid heartbeat, sweating, shaking, difficulty breathing, chest pain)

Because the pandemic increased the feelings of loneliness, isolation, sadness, despair, and anxiety, I want to make a distinction so that you aren't instantly in a panic. The fact that we are all more aware is so good. But please know that the difference between a mental health concern (or crisis) and normal teenage development is the length of time or severity of any of the above symptoms. Our kids feeling sad because they miss their friends or normalcy is different from feeling depressed and hopeless. You know your child best. Keep an eye on them, note behavior changes, and keep communication open as much as possible.

There are many tools and treatments available. Be aware of and support your child. When you suspect help is needed, talk with a mental health professional. The earlier your child learns coping techniques, the easier it will be. I have seen the benefits of therapy with my own kids and with my clients. Teens who have tools and strategies can better manage their flavor of depression and/or anxiety. My daughter Isabelle crochets, employs several breathing techniques, or listens to one of her playlists when her anxiety or depression kicks in. One of my client's sons goes for a run when he feels his depression setting in. Figuring out what works is trial and error. Do not get discouraged. Remember that there are times when your teen may need the care of specialists or may need medication. These are all tools.

Knowing what adolescent mental health looks like is helpful when understanding the mental health of our LGBTQ+ youth. My first stop when I am researching anything related to LGBTQ+ mental health is always The Trevor Project. They provide extremely valuable support in two forms. The first is a 24/7 crisis hotline and chatline (1-866-488-7386). They take calls from youth and parents night and day. I know numerous people who have been saved mentally and physically because The Trevor Project exists. The second valuable form of support from The Trevor Project is the research and information available on their website. I love them and refer people to them daily! I invite you to bookmark, research, and contact The Trevor Project. They exist to support our LGBTQ+ youth!

Though there are incredible challenges for our LGBTQ+ teens there is good news as well. Changes in societal acceptance of LGBTQ+ people have made coming out possible for youth. Compare today's average age of coming out at age sixteen to a decade ago at age eighteen and the 1970s when it was age twenty.[5] Today, the average age of coming out (sixteen) intersects with the developmental period characterized by potentially intense interpersonal and social regulation of gender and sexuality. Given this social/historical context, and despite increasing social acceptance, mental health is a particularly important concern for LGBTQ+ youth.

Connor's mental health journey closely mirrored the statistics shared at the beginning of the chapter regarding mental health for LGBTQ+ adolescents and teens. However, we did not know this when he came out or even when he struggled during his preteen years with anxiety and then with anxiety and depression as a teen and young adult.

Knowledge is half the battle. Solid information helps give us options and allows us to create a plan (or plans) of action. While it doesn't eliminate the trial and error of figuring out the root cause and developing a toolbox of strategies and supports, understanding mental health will definitely point you in the right general direction.

Self-Harm

Self-harm may also appear on your journey, so I want you to know what to look for and what to do. The act of self-harm is purposely causing pain to one's self. It is most typically cutting, burning, scratching, or even binge drinking or unsafe sex. It's important to understand that there is deep turmoil, pain, and perhaps shame that direct self-harm. Those who self-harm feel that by inflicting physical pain, the internal despair will be released.

WHAT TO LOOK FOR

Many times, a person will harm areas of their body that are more difficult to see, such as the upper inner thigh, armpit area, or areas that can be easily covered with clothes.[6] Look for an increase in accidents, long sleeves or pants on hot days, behavior changes, or being more secretive than usual. The most important thing you can do is to respond to your child with compassion and love. Find a professional who specializes in self-harm, and encourage your child to share these complex emotions with a trusted person.

Whenever I bring one of my kids to our pediatrician when they are sick, she first talks to them, checks all the primary symptoms, then turns to me and asks what I think is going on. I have always loved that because, as parents, we know our kids best, even when it feels like we don't.

You know your child. Even if they seem like a stranger at times, the parent-child bond speaks many silent truths. Listen to what is being said between the lines, listen to what your intuition tells you, and advocate for your child if needed.

As you can imagine, the number of our LGBTQ+ kids who are self-harming, including suicide, more than doubles the number of their heterosexual counterparts.[7] Remember, knowledge and truth keep fear in check.

Suicide

At the height of the intensity of our journey, I had one professional tell me that they knew Connor's thoughts better than I did—after only meeting with Connor once! (We did not meet with them again.) For a period of four to five months, we had professionals telling us that Connor's issue was that he was addicted to marijuana. Steve and I fought, persevered, and advocated for him, insisting they dig deeper to find the root cause. Was he smoking to numb the feelings of anxiety and depression, or was it deeper—had he not fully dealt with his coming out process?

A client had a similar experience with their daughter. Within weeks, she went from being involved in activities at school, getting good grades, and living for social time with friends to skipping school and then school refusal. Her parents were shocked and confused, but they knew these behaviors went deeper than rebellion or simple acting out. And they were right! What seemed to be an instant 180 was actually months of internal struggle that their daughter couldn't keep inside any longer and had no clue how to handle. Having these different pieces of the puzzle allowed them to act quickly and seek the help of a therapist.

Suicidal ideation was at play in both of these cases. I know this may feel jarring or frightening, but it is important to understand the difference. Most people think about dying as contemplating our mortality, which is a normal part of living. Ideation is when a person thinks about suicide often and may have a plan of how they may die by suicide. To be clear, according to the National Library of Medicine, ideation is a " . . . broad term used to describe a range of contemplations, wishes, and preoccupations with death and suicide."[8] In some cases, such as with Connor, ideation leads to an attempt. Without going down a rabbit hole to answer the big question—WHY? I want you to know that there are a multitude of studies being conducted to answer this question, as well as offer better ideas for intervention and support for the root causes: pain, hopelessness, connectedness (or lack thereof), and suicide capability.[10]

The statistics don't paint a rosy picture. According to the American Psychological Association and The National Vital Statistics Report, between 2000 and 2021, the suicide rate among youth aged ten to twenty-four rose from 6.8 per 100,000 to 10.7 per 100,000. This rise places suicide as the second leading cause of death for American youth ages ten to fourteen.[9] According to the World Health Organization, "[suicide] was the fourth leading cause of death among 15–29-year-olds globally in 2019."[11]

The Trevor Project shares that LGBTQ+ youth in the US are four times as likely to attempt suicide as their heterosexual and cisgender peers. This equates to 1.8 million LGBTQ+ youth considering suicide every year and one attempt every forty-five seconds.[12]

These numbers are alarming but not surprising. We know the reality our LGBTQ+ kids face. According to The Trevor Project, we know that having "one accepting adult can reduce the risk of a suicide attempt among LGBTQ young people by 40 percent,"[13] but what else can we do?

- We can work to create affirming spaces and activities within our schools and communities.
- We can work to change and create new policies that protect our LGBTQ+ kids from discrimination and other forms of hate.
- We can educate.

I know this is potentially a lot to absorb and may be triggering for some. It is my intent to provide you with studies and statistics so that you feel informed and also to provide personal and actionable steps and tools for supporting our LGBTQ+ kids on an even more personal level. Take a deep breath, and let's look at some tools that can help. The following version of a crisis response plan is one of my favorite tools for two reasons: (1) It is an easy and applicable tool for every one of your loved ones—yourself included, and (2) it works!

The Crisis Response Plan[14] was originally developed in much greater detail for veterans by Dr. Craig Bryan. AnneMoss Rogers revised and shortened Bryan's Crisis Response Plan so that it was universally applicable. While you understand the gravity and importance of this exercise, remember to consider your teen's communication style when introducing the idea. Are they analytical (the more info, the better) or empaths (the more feeling, the better)? Do they like communicating with you through humor, light talks, or intense discussion? Use that information to create space for the creation of this life-saving tool. Offering to create your own version right along with them may help.

Take a large index card and write the answers to the following questions: [15]

1. What are the reasons you like your life? Why do you want to stay here?
2. What is your favorite memory, and what is one thing that reminds you of that memory?
3. Write the name of at least one person you know has your back, no matter what.
4. Write a list of crisis numbers and websites such as:
   » The Trevor Project 866-488-7386
   » US Suicide Hotline 988
   » US/Canada Crisis Text Line 741-741
   » TransLifeLine 877-565-8860

You can make this a family activity. Personalize the card with drawings, colored pens, quotes, or stickers. Most importantly, encourage your child to keep it in a place where they can read it daily.

You know your kid. Just like I always knew that Connor taking a long bath meant depression was overcoming him, you know your child's signs. Don't be afraid to acknowledge those signs or behaviors, speak up, and take action.

I know this can be scary. The feeling of helplessness that parents feel when their child is struggling cannot be described in words. *You are not alone.* There are many options available, including therapy, breathing exercises, helping them find a purpose, and medication. Please know that if your child needs intensive help, it's okay. Shift your thinking from "What did I do wrong?" or "Why is this happening?" to "I am doing everything I can to save my child's life!"

Commit to making one shift today regarding your child's mental health.

You know your child best. Keep an eye on them, note behavior changes, and keep communication open. Remember that the difference between a mental health disorder and typical teenage development is the length of time and severity of any of the above signs or symptoms. Use your journal to note any changes as you observe.

The parent-child bond speaks many silent truths. Listen to what is being said between the lines, listen to what your intuition tells you, and advocate for your child.

Ponder and Reflect

Grab your journal and reflect! Don't overthink it. Just let your thoughts and feelings flow onto the page.

Reflect on your observations about your teen's mental health:

- Where do you think they struggle?
- What do they seem to handle in a healthy way?
- Assess where they need support.
- Create a Crisis Response Plan with your teen.

CHAPTER TEN

Be Alert to Substance Abuse

The best way out is always through.

—ROBERT FROST

When Connor first came out, and I began my research journey, I was really thrown by how often LGBTQ+ mental health and substance use and abuse were discussed simultaneously. It took me a while to fully understand the connection. Up to that point, I had a hardline stance on any substances, alcohol included: zero tolerance until my kids were of age. Boy, did I have a lot to learn—and a lot of breathing to do!

The problem with how we handled zero tolerance is that there was pretty much no discussion or education around it. Steve has always been more laid back about it, but I was beyond rigid. The discussion was "Vodka will kill you, smoking is bad, marijuana is a gateway drug, drugs will kill you—end of discussion." So, I started this portion of our journey by first having to unlearn and then begin my education.

Like the chapter on mental health, let's begin with an overview of substance abuse for adolescents, teens, and young adults in general and then hone in on our LGBTQ+ kids specifically. It is not surprising that, more often than not, substance use and abuse go hand-in-hand with mental health disorders, specifically depression and anxiety.

Commonly called co-occurring disorders or dual diagnosis, the National Institute on Drug Abuse has found that 60 percent of teens struggling with substance use also struggle with a mental health disorder.[1]

The human brain, specifically the frontal lobe, continues developing from adolescence into early adulthood (around age twenty-five). This is why you may be puzzled by how extraordinarily smart your teen is one minute, but you may not recognize them the next. Decision-making and impulse control are just two of the many mental and physical functions the frontal lobe controls. Our teens are literally biologically wired to take risks and experiment.

Knowing that both mental health disorders and substance abuse have roots in one's biology, genetics, psychology, and environment helps us grasp the enormity of these issues and understand why there is not a one-size-fits-all solution. Teen substance use and abuse go beyond alcohol consumption and marijuana use. It also includes both over-the-counter and prescription medications, hallucinogens, and vaping. In fact, according to the 2021 Youth Risk Behavior Survey conducted by the Centers for Disease Control and Prevention, 22.7 percent of high school-aged kids responded they currently drank alcohol, 15.8 percent currently used marijuana, and 12.2 percent currently took prescription medication that was not prescribed to them.[2]

Teens are more sophisticated in their use than they were even a decade ago, making it much more difficult to simply smell any substance on them. If you are concerned and they have passed the smell test, here is an essential list of signs that your teen may be using substances:

- red eyes or constricted pupils
- flushed cheeks
- hysterical laughter or loud, nonsensical behavior
- unusual clumsiness
- repeatedly missing curfew
- becoming secretive about their plans or vague plans

If you see any of these signs or suspect drug use, the next big question is, should you search their room? The teenage years are a delicate dance of respecting their growing need for privacy while maintaining communication and keeping them safe. It is developmentally appropriate for them to begin to pull away, close their bedroom doors, and test boundaries as they move toward independence. The thought of intruding on their space or violating their privacy may create a mental dilemma for you. So, to search or not to search? It is actually quite simple. If you are concerned about your teen's safety, search away; it doesn't matter whether they have ten signs on the door telling you to stay out. They live under your roof, and their health and safety are your number one priority.

I say that now because of what I have been through. It never occurred to me to search Connor's room. He had always been a rule follower, a pleaser, and an overachiever in everything he did—until he wasn't. His incredible intelligence allowed him the ability to be a master manipulator. It was almost too late when we realized our darling boy was brilliant at living two lives.

The first time I found substances in Connor's room was by complete accident. It was the beginning of summer, a few months after he had come out to us, and I was looking for water bottles. I swear they are like socks and spoons—they just disappear into thin air. His was the last room I searched, and as I looked under his bathroom sink, I hit the jackpot. Unfortunately, not water bottles, but one far more revealing: a homemade bong and an Altoids box filled with marijuana. I remember standing there, stunned, altogether abandoning my prior hunt. It was one of those moments when time slows and whips around you like an inferno.

As my shock slowly morphed into sadness, then fear, and finally anger, I got the courage to look in drawers, under his bed, and in his closet. I had a neat collection of a vape pen, vape cartridges, and a Gatorade bottle filled with alcohol by the time I was finished. While I felt so alone in that moment, I have come to hear similar versions of this story from so many other parents. Whether it is experimentation or a piece of your child's bigger puzzle, the best (and hardest!) thing to do is seek answers. A careful search of their personal spaces is a starting point for conversation and getting support or intervention if needed.

Are you wondering what to look for or where to look? Here are some places to begin:

- mint boxes or tins; candy containers
- any plastic bottle—do NOT assume the liquid is water
- duffle or gym bags
- shoeboxes
- inside books
- sock drawers: INSIDE the socks
- inside the water tank of the toilet
- shampoo (etc.) bottles
- pockets of off-season gear (like winter coats if it's summer)
- inside makeup cases
- buried in the dirt of indoor plants
- under loose floorboards

Interestingly, a study called Project Self-Discovery was recently conducted in Iceland, which twenty years ago had the highest rate of youth substance use and abuse. This study offered teenagers natural-high alternatives to drugs. For kids seeking a rush, project researchers found that giving them a risk-taking but safe alternative, like skateboarding or skiing, could replace the synthetic high offered by drugs with a natural high. For kids who prefer the sedative effect of a depressant, they found that introducing them to yoga or running could produce a similar effect. This fascinating study showed that kids are not necessarily addicted to the substance but to the release of the hormones that create the desired feeling.[3]

Following the pattern of increased mental health disorders in LGBTQ+ teens, substance use and abuse also increase in LGBTQ+ teens. It doesn't require a degree in psychology to understand why. In addition to the regular growing pains of adolescence, coming to realize that they are gay, lesbian, bisexual, transgender, or queer adds a confusion-filled layer that is often wrought with fear, shame, denial, anger, and isolation.

More often than not, they turn to some kind of self-medication to numb the overwhelming pounding of emotion and reality. In fact, data released by The Substance Abuse and Mental Health Services Administration (SAMHSA) found that:

> Lesbian and bisexual females were more likely than straight females to have engaged in binge drinking in the past month, and about twice as likely to have engaged in heavy drinking in the past month. Gay and bisexual males and females were two to three times more likely than their straight counterparts to have used illicit drugs other than marijuana in the past year. [and] Bisexual females were three times more likely than straight females to have had an opioid use disorder in the past year.[4]

There is no adequate research on substance use in transgender teens at this time, but based on anecdotal evidence, concern is warranted.

Club drugs, hallucinogens, and stimulants, including MDMA (Ecstasy or Molly) and methamphetamine (crystal meth or Tina), are more prevalent with LGBTQ+ teens than with their heterosexual peers. Please do your homework and talk to your kids because these drugs are far more commonplace with our LGBTQ+ teens and young adults.

It is *essential* to understand that being LGBTQ+ does **NOT** cause substance abuse. Rather, the weight of their coming out process and the pressures and messages they are receiving from their world drive them to find a way to block it all. Potential root causes for substance use can include but are not limited to bullying and harassment, family conflict and rejection, minority stress, childhood abuse, and gender stereotypes.

Understanding, knowing what to look for, and asking questions help us provide the support they need to avoid substances. Professional guidance may be particularly helpful here if you are feeling frozen or, conversely, like everything is out of control.

Keeping lines of communication open will help too. Even if the conversation or exchange of words is only a minute or two long, that is long enough for you to assess what may or may not be going on, AND it is long enough for them to energetically connect with you—even if verbally it feels like they are rejecting you. By energetically, I mean the unspoken connection we share with our kids. We are all energetic beings—sometimes connecting on that level is more powerful than with words. No teen wants to discuss substance use with their parents (sex and dating also fall in this category); HOWEVER, it is one of those uncomfortable necessities. The double bonus of having this conversation is that not only are you offering valuable, no-nonsense education, but you are also letting them know you know what's up. When information is shared factually without judgment, our adolescents, teens, and young adults are much more willing to listen.

Before you go into this conversation, make sure you (and your spouse/partner) are clear on the values and rules you want to convey. As much as most of our kids will push the envelope on rules and break them from time to time, seemingly without remorse, study after study shows that they feel more confident and secure knowing rules are in place.[5] In fact, knowing that, I encourage you to have conversations explaining WHY you value and believe what you do. Again, even if the outward reaction is eyes rolling and a wall, internally, they value what you think and believe, and it WILL make a difference in their decision-making.

Remember, open-ended questions are always best; if you can, try to pique their curiosity. For example, instead of saying, "Even though marijuana is natural, it's not safe, and you shouldn't use it," try, "Tell me what you know about marijuana." And you can even follow it up with, "Do you think it is safe? Why or why not?" And so on.

I know this next part may sound silly, but I promise it makes a difference—words really do matter! Word choice is generational and geographical above all, meaning our age and location are a subtle guide for our word choice. It is totally fine to joke around with your kids using their lingo, but when you are having more serious conversations, you need to find the fine line of language that doesn't make you sound ninety but also doesn't make you sound like you are trying too hard. It's that sweet spot where they think, "Wow, Mom (or Dad) really knows what they're talking about—and they want to know what I think too!"

As your teen navigates high school, there is a high likelihood that they will find themselves in at least one situation where peer pressure is an issue or they just feel uncomfortable. Come up with a code word that they can text you that means you will come to pick them up, no questions asked. Additionally, I have implemented the *blame-mom rule*: if they are unable to text for whatever reason, put it on me, as in "my mom always figures everything out—she'll ground me for a month." A little exaggeration is okay. One of my favorite stories is from a client who implemented the blame-mom rule with her daughter. Her daughter was able to use it effectively to remove herself from situations such as parties where there was alcohol. Then, her friends started using it, too, saying that if my client found out, she would tell their moms too. While we do not want our kids to lean on this crutch indefinitely, it is a helpful stepping stone to implement while they are developing.

Know that substance use and abuse is something every parent of a teen needs to be educated on. Understand that our LGBTQ+ kids are at higher risk—not because being LGBTQ+ causes it, but because of the intensity of their unique coming out process. Keep in mind what to look for, but most importantly, remember that having open, honest conversations is the best prevention and redirection.

Ponder and Reflect

Grab your journal and reflect! Don't overthink it. Just let your thoughts and feelings flow onto the page.

- Brainstorm a few questions you could ask your kids that are open-ended and will keep communication open.
- Talk with your spouse or partner about the rules and values you want to convey. It is super important to be on the same page. Use your journal to come up with a few values you and your partner can agree on.
- This is also an excellent time to decide on your approach. Journal some code word options or practice a few blame-mom tactics with your child.

CHAPTER ELEVEN

Adjust to Your New Reality

Daring to set boundaries is about having the courage to love ourselves even when we risk disappointing others.

—BRENÉ BROWN

I had just sunk onto my couch with a cup of tea and a book, happy to have a quiet house and a few minutes to unwind before bed, when I heard the noise. I had already said goodnight to Steve and all four of my kids, and my dog was sprawled on the couch next to me. I tiptoed upstairs and saw a light from underneath Connor's door. Standing there quietly, I heard the sound of his window opening. Anger surged through me. *Nope*, I thought, *not this time.* I quietly walked back downstairs and went outside through the patio door, making my way around the house to stand underneath his second-floor bedroom window. As I stood there, tapping my nails on my teacup, he popped his head out of the window, looked down the street, and threw out a rope. I waited until he was halfway out before I said, "Going somewhere?"

This sliver of our story shows the adjustment to a new reality and the need for revised rules and boundaries—with Connor and others in my life. I went from having no clue what a boundary was to realizing they were a necessity!

Setting Boundaries 101

Setting boundaries is a process. In chapter seven, I described the what, why, and how of boundaries. In this chapter, we are going to take a deeper look. Remember, a healthy boundary is a physical, emotional, or abstract line that clearly communicates what behaviors are acceptable to you.

Why set healthy boundaries? Boundaries are a vital form of self-care, and they communicate how you wish to be treated by others, as well as your needs and wants.

How do you set healthy boundaries? Setting healthy boundaries begins within. Recognize that you are worthy of respect.

This process is personal and entirely your own. It involves practicing your favorite forms of self-care, which will help you process all this new information. It also involves being gentle with yourself, your child, and your family as you experience expansions and contractions. And it involves learning to not only set but also adjust boundaries. Remember, boundaries are not exclusive to parents! Teaching your children about boundaries and how to set them will help them positively navigate relationships their entire lives.

The purpose of setting a healthy boundary is to protect and take care of **you**. It is a very personal practice as it is based on your unique needs and wants. Looking at the story from the beginning of the chapter, the boundary created was twofold: please adhere to our rules and please be respectful of me as a human being. In setting this boundary and discussing it with Connor, he, in turn, learned why boundaries are important and how to set them for his unique needs.

The first step in creating healthy boundaries is to have self-compassion. If this is completely new to you (like it was to me), you may be thinking, *Oh my goodness, what in the world is that?* Don't fret. Self-compassion is one more self-care tool that is easy to implement; it requires awareness and practice. And, when you model self-compassion for your kids, they can see and feel how it benefits you and them! What a great way to teach by doing!

Self-compassion can be thought of in terms of the yin and the yang—the yin is the comforting, soothing, and validating we do for ourselves; the yang is the protecting, providing, and motivating we do out in the world.[1] It is nurturing and kindness toward self, as well as inner strength and protective actions toward oneself. It is learning to separate behavior from self-worth, in other words, realizing that you are a human with flaws who may occasionally behave badly, but that behavior does not define you.

According to Jo Nash in *Positive Psychology*, the benefits of healthy boundaries are good mental health, good emotional health, developed autonomy, developed identity, avoidance of burnout, and influence on others' behavior.[2]

So, the big question is, how do we set healthy boundaries?

1. Examine where boundaries currently exist and do not exist and decide where you need them most. What do you want in the various relationships in your life?

2. Say what you need or DO NOT need. Remember, "no" is a complete sentence. Be clear.

3. Super important—keep it simple. Not over explaining or giving a list of reasons is crucial to setting healthy boundaries. You have the right to decide what you want to do or not do. Keep the focus on you and your needs, not the other person or situation.

4. Finally, say why it is important to you and set consequences you are willing to follow through on.

Healthy boundaries can be the difference between a loving, respectful relationship and a toxic, dysfunctional one.

If you are new to setting healthy boundaries, know it will initially feel awkward. You may feel like you are being selfish or even mean. I've been there, and those feelings still pop in occasionally when I'm re-setting or firming up boundaries I have been working to put in place. Know that not everyone will respond with delight that you are taking care of your mental health and well-being or that of your family. You may have people in your life who are chronic boundary hoppers. When this happens, return to your reasoning and repeat the above steps. Remember, taking care of yourself ultimately allows you to be the best version of yourself for YOU and for everyone around you who matters most.

By setting healthy boundaries, you give yourself the space you need to fully absorb what you are learning; space to experience the journey that you, your child, and your family are on; and space to stretch, evolve, and grow.

Take the time now; it will pay off in beautiful ways down the road.

Here are a few examples of boundaries that you may set:

- saying "no" to anything you don't want to do
- making expectations or rules clear
- honoring your emotions and the emotions of others
- having honest, clear conversations
- expressing your needs and wants, do not assume others will figure them out

Here are a few examples of boundaries that you can encourage your teen to set:

- asking for family members to respect their privacy—this need is developmentally appropriate and necessary as they prepare to individuate [Note, if you feel your teen is unsafe or may have illegal items in their room or spaces, those concerns take priority—you may need to search their room, and that is okay.]
- saying "no" to anything that they don't want to do within peer relationships
- using what healthy communication feels like to them (i.e., where they feel respected) as a guide

One type of boundary that often comes up for parents of LGBTQ+ kids, as well as LGBTQ+ kids, is around safety. This will look different for everyone, but here are a few basic concepts and guidelines to keep in mind.

- We can create a safe environment in our home. When we create a place where our kids feel seen and heard, they feel safe.

It builds their confidence and allows them to go out into the world.

- We can advocate for them at school, in the community, and in the world. Doing this creates a verbal boundary over and over of what behaviors are okay. Our kids see us, and they will model in their own way.

- We can create the rules and boundaries in our homes. The more specific, the better. And, know that over time, they will shift and change as your family grows. Assuming our kids would continue the path of respecting our general household rules instead of being very specific and consistent as they entered the teenage years was one of the biggest mistakes we made, and that mistake led to Connor sneaking out of his window!

Adjusting our parenting from childhood to adolescence to the teen years is an adventure, to say the least. Every child is different, and the approach for each will change over time. The rules we set when our kids are young will obviously change over time. Focus on the specificity of these changing rules and discuss them regularly with your children. Allow space for questions and for clarifying or tweaking as necessary.

The rules and boundaries you create may not be perfect the first time. That's okay. The more discussion that occurs, the better everyone will have a clear understanding. Being flexible and allowing for adjustment to figure out what works best for you and your family will also help you recalibrate.

Balance

While we all have commonalities, this journey is unique to you and your family. It is not a race. There is no finish line. Do the work to be present, breathe in the beautiful moments, and sit through the uncomfortable ones.

A while back, I had the opportunity to interview Kirsten Beverley-Waters, author of *The Struggle Guru*. One of the highlights for me was our discussion on the chapter called, "Compass You Are."[3] The analogy and the lessons offered based on that analogy have helped me make profound shifts in my life. Kirsten shares in her book, "Your compass is likely broken. It could be the needle, or an inadvertent miscalculation of your north...[the] poet Rumi teaches us that when we do as others say, we become blind, and when we come when others call, we become lost."[4] Pretty direct. So, how do we know if our compass is broken?

Over time, I've seen many different versions of the compass analogy. Each one teaches a system for balance and aligning with your authentic self. For example, the compass analogy begins with finding your true north, your authentic self, your purpose. The road you travel to find your purpose is unique to you. You may have completed this journey early in life, or you may be on it into mid and later life. Your choices, personal work, and commitment to connecting with and living your life's purpose are all pavers on this path.

Spirituality brings balance to the authentic self. It is shaped by your belief system, connections to, and understanding of consciousness or a power greater than yourself. Remember, spirituality does not equal religion. The True self is rooted in your spirituality. Other versions refer to this as Om and South.

In the compass analogy, East and West symbolize external experiences, environment, and internal wisdom. External experiences include where you live, your access to education, where you have traveled, people you have met, your job, the energy surrounding you, and so on. Internal wisdom is gained from your external experiences and environment. Other versions are more specific about external experiences, including and detailing the influence of work, family and friend relationships, and lifestyle.

As you think of each of these examples, the yin and the yang may come to mind, or even perhaps a scale. Use whatever visual works best for you to create balance in all areas of your life.

Imbalance can present in many different ways. Perhaps you are not connected to your authentic self or your life's purpose, or maybe you are on a spiritual journey. It could also present as seeking validation or a sense of self from external experiences or interactions instead of allowing that information to be nourishment for your internal wisdom.[5]

Just like learning to create and set boundaries, finding balance takes time and patience. Whether you feel like the needle of your compass is spinning or you have steadily been following your true north your whole life, I want you to take some time analyzing each area of your life. Having a deep understanding of each will help you experience and be present in this journey with your child. The added bonus of balance is that it helps you stay connected to your intuition. (More on this to come in chapter fourteen.)

Ponder and Reflect

Grab your journal and reflect! Don't overthink it. Just let your thoughts and feelings flow onto the page.

- Boundaries involve nurturing, kindness, inner strength, and protective actions toward oneself. Setting them involves learning to separate behavior from self-worth. You are human! How does this make you feel?
- Where do you need boundaries in your life?
- Be clear about what you do and DO NOT need/want.
- Keep it simple.
- Say why the boundary is important to YOU.
- How can you incorporate the comforting, soothing, and validating aspects of Yin Self-Compassion with the protecting, providing, and motivating aspects of Yang Self-Compassion?

Action Steps for Pillar Two: Educate and Unlearn Bias

- Where do you think your child is in their coming out process? In what ways can you support them?
- Where are you in your coming out process? What information or support would be helpful?
- What do you need when it comes to specific support from family, friends, spirituality, professionals, and your community?
- Assess what your child's mental health needs are.
- If you have concerns about substance use, what information and support would be helpful?
- Check in with yourself and look ahead.
- Where are you right now? Record your goals.
    » One-week goal
    » One-month goal
    » One-year goal

· · · · ·

This is not a race . . . there is no deadline. Be gentle with yourself and your child as you adjust to your new reality. Change is not necessarily bad; we resist it because it is unknown. Take that first gentle step to unlearn your biases. With each step forward, and every new piece of knowledge, your mind will expand and you will grow as a human being. And remember . . . you are not alone!

Pillar Three:
Empower

*A*mong my favorite topics are learning to empower and be empowered, to advocate for and be an advocate, and to be an ally. Empowering is both freeing and grounding. It is loving and fierce. It is open-hearted and protective. It makes sense that this is the third pillar, because to truly activate it, we need to fully embrace our child and this journey and be actively educating ourselves.

The dictionary definition of empower is "[to] make (someone) stronger and more confident, especially in controlling their life and claiming their rights."[1]

One of our top priorities as parents is empowering our children to shine in the world authentically. We can only fully achieve that if we have empowered ourselves. So what actions can we take to become empowered and then to empower? In this pillar, we'll work to fully understand empowerment, explore how communication is vital, talk about trusting our intuition, and discover the importance of releasing any fear.

CHAPTER TWELVE

Empower and Be Empowered

Don't be afraid. Be focused. Be determined.
Be hopeful. Be empowered.

—MICHELLE OBAMA

The first step in empowerment is knowledge. In the second pillar, we focused on learning about the coming out process, finding the right support, and preparing for potential mental health and substance abuse challenges. Those are important topics, and there will likely be hurdles unique to your journey along the way. You will encounter inaccurate or outdated information. You may struggle to find information on your specific topic. The magic keyword combination to access what you are looking for online will elude you. A little patience and a lot of deep breaths will yield many benefits.

Empower Through Education

There isn't a *right* or a *best* way to learn; you can choose the avenues that best suit your learning style. For instance, if you love to read, then books, websites, and articles are good choices. If you learn by interaction, speaking with professionals, attending parent meetings, and participating in LGBTQ+ events are more up your alley. If you like to learn as you multitask, or if you are an auditory learner, then podcasts, audiobooks, and TedTalks are a great option.

As this chapter's quote suggests, hope and empowerment are possible as we learn new information. Strategies for overcoming obstacles, coping techniques for overwhelm, stigma-busting information, and clarity are closer than you may realize. Is there misinformation out there? Absolutely! However, if you use my tips and list as a guide, you will steer clear of the inaccuracies and harmful ideologies. The more you take in new information in whatever form suits you best, the better you will be able to spot the nonsense for yourself.

Another benefit, and the reason we all invest our time and energy into researching, is that learning gives us an opportunity to learn who our children are, understand what they are experiencing, and get clarity about the current climate for the LGBTQ+ community.

Many techniques and tools are available to empower you and help you empower others. The following five are my favorites for becoming empowered. These are the ones I use on repeat!

TOOLS TO EMPOWER OURSELVES

1. **Education:** There is a reason the education pillar precedes the empower pillar. As I said multiple times, knowledge is power. Being educated on a subject helps us stay calm, create a plan, or move more smoothly throughout our lives.

2. **Self-care:** Not surprisingly, when we nurture our own needs in the ways that our bodies, minds, and souls need at that moment, we create the foundation for self-empowerment. Being empowered includes feeling grounded and secure, and only our personal self-care formula can provide that. Teaching our children the importance of self-care and finding what works best for them does two critical things. First, it models looking inward for one's needs rather than seeking external validation. Second, by learning how to nurture their bodies, minds, and souls, our children go out into the world feeling confident and, you've got it, empowered.

3. **Be open to possibilities:** It is easy to get stuck in our routines, doing what is comfortable and known day after day. While there is something to be said about the grounding power of a routine, there is a sweet spot in that formula. Acknowledging, allowing, and being open to possibilities and opportunities is a simple and gentle way to empower yourself. Try new and different things, even when you think you're not good at them, and encourage your child to do the same.

4. **Focus on who you are:** Trust yourself. Love what you do, and find purpose and passion. This is more of a mantra mixed with a goal. Focus on who you are at your core. Trust who you are— your instinct, your intuition, and your core beliefs. Allow this focus and trust to guide you to help you find your purpose and your passion. When you are connected to a purpose, empowerment follows. Our kids are already generationally better at this than we are, and it is a wonderful trait to acknowledge in them and encourage them to connect with as they grow.

5. **Allow yourself to be human:** The final tool is to be gentle with yourself. Embrace the beauty in the messiness and the imperfection! Look at failures, flaws, and mistakes as opportunities to learn and become a better, stronger, and more resilient version of yourself. Change your self-talk from "I can't do it" to "I can't do it YET—but I can learn."

When my kids were much younger, I would read books and articles about empowering children and helping them build confidence and resilience. Employing the techniques I was learning about seemed light-years away or, in some cases, unnecessary. Well, suffice it to say, I have pulled out many of those books over the past few years and worked to sharpen my empowerment skills.

For the sake of simplicity and to reduce overwhelm, I have wrapped my favorite empowering techniques and tools into five actionable suggestions that are applicable to our LGBTQ+ loves, as well as ourselves.

TOOLS FOR EMPOWERING YOUR KIDS

1. **Give your child choices:** I don't mean allow them to run your house or give them lists of dozens of activities to choose from;

rather, hone in on their strengths or areas you think they may enjoy exploring, then present two to three choices. Additionally, allow them to take risks—not life-threatening ones, but risks that will challenge them and allow them to grow. Encourage your child to follow their interests. When an adolescent or young adult has a passion or purpose they are pursuing, their mental health improves, and that overflows into every other area of their life, empowering them to continue stretching and growing.

2. **Let them fail:** Mistakes are powerful teachers. Empowering also means giving our children the space to make mistakes and learn from them. By letting them fail and supporting them through the process, we teach them to embrace a growth mindset. Each mistake or failure can translate into learning. This type of learning builds resilience and an empowered child!

3. **Listen to your child:** We will look at this more closely in the next chapter, but know for now that actively listening and being present establishes trust. That trust sends the message that they are safe, further empowering them.

4. **Teach your child body safety:** I have found that approaching this one casually and matter-of-factly works well. Keep in mind it is a topic that you will want to discuss more than once. Depending on what age you introduce it, you will want to continue adding to the conversation as your child moves through the teen years and into adulthood. Body safety is teaching respect and love for one's body, as well as the importance of healthy boundaries and healthy relationships. Body safety involves discussing different age-appropriate scenarios of feeling safe versus feeling unsafe, as well as what to do in those instances where they do not feel safe.

5. **Choose and use your words wisely:** Words and actions matter. I grew up in a home where my parents used words and actions without considering the effect on my siblings or me. I am drawn to this tool because I know firsthand the negative consequences. Long before Connor came out or I discovered my life purpose, Steve and I parented very consciously, especially when it came to words and actions. This is also where modeling

the behavior and habits we want our children to learn comes in. When we are conscious about our word choice, own up to our mistakes, and not only allow but encourage our children to be part of the process, we empower them in multiple ways.

Learning and using accurate words and phrases is a vital part of your child's process, as well as your own. It is part of validating their experience and who they are. Ask them open-ended questions about words or phrases you don't know or don't understand. They will love that you asked, and it is an opening for an enlightening conversation—regardless of whether they have the correct answer. The reference section at the back of this book includes definitions for many LGBTQ+ words and terms to help you choose your words wisely.

Advocate and Ally—Nouns and Verbs

I am a writer and a total grammar nerd at heart. So, letting you in on my love affair with the dual meanings (and pronunciations) of the word *advocate* seems like a fair admission at this point. Of course, my love for this word stems from the strength and beauty it represents for ALL of our kids, especially our LGBTQ+ loves. Including it in this chapter just seems to make perfect sense, right? One cannot advocate or be an advocate without first being empowered.

For fun, I want to share the Cambridge Dictionary definition of both:

Noun—advocate—someone who publicly supports someone or something.[1]

Verb—to advocate—the act of publicly supporting or suggesting an idea, development, or way of doing something.[2]

Our kids need us to be both! The more we learn, grow, and empower ourselves and our children, the better prepared we will be to advocate and to be an advocate when needed. And just in case you are wondering, being an LGBTQ+ *ally* is just that! Being an ally is not just who you are; it is the action you take daily as you advocate for your child. Here is a list of actions an ally might take:

- Learn LGBTQ+ history.
- Listen—with the intent to learn not with the intent to respond.

- Educate yourself on common LGBTQ+ language and issues.
- Take a stand. Speak up, sign petitions, and participate in protests and parades.
- Celebrate Pride Month—attend parades, volunteer, stand in solidarity.
- Challenge anti-LGBTQ+ speech.
- Leverage your influence and privilege to promote inclusion and equity.
- Be aware of your biases; actively work through them; apologize when necessary.
- Learn from your mistakes.
- Create a safe space for your child and their friends.

Ponder and Reflect

Grab your journal and reflect! Don't overthink it. Just let your thoughts and feelings flow onto the page.

Empower: [to] make someone stronger and more confident, especially in controlling their life and claiming their rights.

- What actions can you take to become empowered?
- What actions can you take to empower your child?
- List a few ways you can be an *advocate* for your child, as well as ways you can *advocate* for the LGBTQ community.

CHAPTER THIRTEEN

Communicate

The way we talk to our children
becomes their inner voice.

—PEGGY O'MARA

he advent of the internet and social media has undoubtedly been both a blessing and a curse. I believe that there are more benefits than detriments for those of us who are over forty. We learned face-to-face communication skills, as well as all the joys (lol!) of researching in books only and handwriting everything in our teen and young adult years! Our kids, on the other hand, have had the internet and social media for most of their lives. Having instant access to information (both true and false), their friends, entertainment, etc., has created a whole new world for all of us, parent and child alike, to navigate. Creating boundaries around usage and content, having discussions about communication, and teaching that not everything online and on social media is true are just a few of the areas that are brand new territory.

I believe the biggest casualty of the internet and social media has been human interaction. Our kids are missing out on learning the nuances of communication, so our job of filling the communication gap has become much more important. Helping our kids learn to carry on a conversation and to work through disagreements are two ways to begin filling that gap.

Talk Time

Make time to talk with and connect with your teen daily. Everyone is busy, so you must prioritize that time. It can be as simple as a two-minute check-in. I have always loved one-on-one car time because kids are much more likely to relax and open up when there isn't the pressure of eye contact. It's also the captive audience idea.

If that isn't an option, or your child is already driving, you can try asking them to be your sous chef while you make dinner, or you can ask for tech help with your phone or your computer and just go with the flow of conversation. One of my favorites is starting a conversation with "I read the other day [fill in the blank with an uncomfortable topic]. What do you think of that?" Extra points if you say you saw it on TikTok! The point is to *create* opportunities to communicate and to connect.

TALK ABOUT CURRENT EVENTS

I like this one for so many reasons. When you approach it as a conversation, not a lecture, you signal that you are interested in what they know, as well as what they are curious about. The underlying bonus is that you learn what they are learning in school, as well as what they are picking up from social media or friends. Allowing them to discuss and ask questions about local, national, and world events allows two cool things to happen: 1. It helps them develop critical thinking skills and form their own opinions. 2. It allows you to share your thoughts and beliefs in a conversational way. Our kids want to know what we think, but they don't want to be talked at. Have you ever gotten lost in telling a story or sharing an idea that you feel passionately about only to look over and see your teen staring off into space or glazing over with that I'm-so-bored look? I certainly have! This is why I love this tip. It allows you to share in a way that is captivating for your teen.

THE SKILL OF SMALL TALK

It may seem weird that this is in the section for healthy communication, but stick with me for a minute. Do you remember your first professional events or parties with different groups of friends where you were thrust into conversations with strangers? Perhaps this was a breeze for you—or maybe it was an anxiety-attack-inducing nightmare! Learning how to navigate small talk and mastering the art of active listening are vital for simple interactions and for healthy relationships. So how do we help our kids develop this skill, thus empowering them? We model it. When you find yourself in light topic conversation, make a recap statement with a follow-up question every minute or two or when there is a natural break in the conversation. Obviously, this is a super subtle way of teaching the art of small talk, but it is far less awkward than making a big deal about it and potentially making it more stressful. And it is something you likely naturally do already without thinking about it. An example of a simple exchange could be the following:

"How was your afternoon at the beach?"

Whether their answer is one word or one hundred, stay engaged and stay present. Perhaps your teen shares that it was nice and sunny and, among other things, their friend hates their new summer job. At an appropriate pause, say:

"It sounds like it was perfect summer weather. I'm sorry your friend doesn't like their summer job. That's a bummer."

You're showing—and teaching—good listening skills, empathy, and simple ways to create a back-and-forth conversation.

Navigating Disagreements

Disagreements happen. They are part of life and part of relationships. Through plenty of life experience, I have learned that how disagreements are handled and resolved is one of the most prominent signs of the health and functionality of a relationship.

USE "I" STATEMENTS

One of the best tools I've learned in the past decade is to use I statements when talking about my feelings or a situation. For example, say, "I feel frustrated when you (fill in the blank)" instead of "You frustrate me."

Making this subtle change does two things: first, it states clearly what you are frustrated about, and second, it eliminates blame which typically will either ignite or shut down the person you are frustrated with.

TRY USING VAST: VALIDATE, ASK, SEE, TALK

My favorite tool for cultivating positive and healthy communication is a method I created. It is not rocket science by any means, but I have found that the acronym makes it easier to remember. It is called the *VAST method*. It stands for *Validate*, *Ask* questions, *See* them, then— and only then—*Talk*. Let's break it all down.

VALIDATE

Validating involves being aware of someone's feelings and acknowledging those feelings as important. If you are new to validating, don't worry; while it is a bit awkward at first, with a little practice, you'll be a pro in no time. Steve and I first learned the concept of validation when Connor was at the therapeutic boarding school. There are three steps:

1. Listen and respond in simple ways, such as nodding or saying "okay" or "uh-huh," so they know you are listening.
2. Show that you are present and listening with body language such as eye contact, turning toward the person, etc.
3. After they have finished expressing their feelings, repeat their words back to them and affirm the feeling they have expressed. I know this sounds silly, but it lets them know you heard and understood them.

Here is an example of validating: My daughter came home from school one day and was not herself. She is seventeen, and although, at times, it can take a little coaxing to get her talking, once she's going, I often get to relive the situation in real time. So, on this particular afternoon, I learned she had been left out of plans with a group of kids she considered friends. Now, validating can get a little tricky if the story you are being told is long, so steps one and two are super important. Eye contact, positive body language, and an "okay" or "oh my" work. Once she finished sharing, it was time for step three. I gently said, "I understand that they didn't include you in their plans, and that made you really sad. Is that right?" That final "Is that right?" allows your child to correct anything you may have misunderstood.

Understanding the opposite of validating helps because it is something we all do as parents. What is our automatic response when our child is in pain or struggling? We want to fix it, right? It is at that moment when you are opening your mouth to fix that you will build the awareness to close it and listen! Steve is a big fixer. During a recent conversation with Connor, Steve was doing his best to fix a problem he was struggling with. Connor got so exasperated that he finally yelled, "I just want to know that you are hearing me!" Whoa! Lightbulb moment. Our kids just want—and need—for us to confirm that we hear them and that we understand (or are at least trying to understand). Learning to simply validate takes work and practice, but if we can do it, so can you!

ASK QUESTIONS

Once you have validated your teen's feelings, ask this very important question before saying or doing anything else: "Do you want me to listen and reflect, or would you also like to know what I think?" The answer to this question will let you know what kind of clarifying questions you can ask or what information you can offer. Either way, this signals to your child that you want to understand, AND it allows you time to pause internally if what is being shared rattles you in any way. Here are a few options for follow-up questions: What do *you* want to do? If there were no consequences, what would you want to say? What makes you most frustrated about this situation?

SEE THEM

Be present. Hold their hand, rub their back, or hug them (if they respond positively to physical touch). Breathe into focusing wholly on them in that moment. This is SO huge. Really seeing our children for who they inherently are requires us to remove all of our expectations and movie-reel creations. Breathe through the discomfort. I love this quote by Jeff Brown that says in part, "To feel seen in our humanity, in our vulnerability, in our beautiful imperfection . . . if there is anything we can offer each other, it is the gift of sight. 'I see you' [are] perhaps the most important words we can utter to another."

If your child finally feels comfortable enough to open up to you and talk, do NOT ruin it by checking your phone or allowing yourself to be distracted by the ding or vibration of an incoming text. One slip can cause them to shut down again. Unless you are an on-call doctor, nothing on your phone is a life-or-death matter.

THEN—AND ONLY THEN—TALK

When it's time to talk, remember first your child's response to that important question "Do you want me to listen and reflect, or would you also like to know what I think?" Allow their response to guide you. If they want your thoughts and advice, be thoughtful and gentle. If they just want you to listen, tell them you love them and thank them for trusting you and confiding in you.

When your child feels validated, seen, and heard—oh my goodness—their confidence will deepen, and the trust and understanding in your relationship will develop and grow in ways you may never have imagined. They will truly feel and be empowered!

Ponder and Reflect

Grab your journal and reflect! Don't overthink it. Just let your thoughts and feelings flow onto the page.

- I challenge you to try one of the techniques from this chapter, as well as the VAST method. Write down which you're going to try and why you think it will work best.
- Reflect in your journal after each try of a new technique and note what works and doesn't work for you and your child, as well as what you want to try differently next time.

CHAPTER FOURTEEN

Lean into Your Intuition

The more you trust your intuition,
the more empowered you become, the stronger
you become, the happier you become.

—GISELE BÜNDCHEN

Have you ever had a gentle nudging of a feeling that you should or should not do something? Or maybe you've been on a walk or meditating, and a fabulous idea just popped into your head. You may think of it as instinct, energy, or purpose. Whatever name you want to give it, it is, at the core, your incredible intuition!

Trust Your Intuition

Did you know there are tools, strategies, and practices that help us to become aware of and learn to trust this powerful inner voice? When we learn to lean into instead of questioning our intuition, our sense of empowerment deepens. We learn to trust ourselves and make confident decisions. We learn to look inward for answers. We become aware of all our senses. And doing so allows us to radiate empowerment to others.

My journey of discovering and learning to trust my intuition has been quite bumpy. I think I have always been aware of the guiding voice within, but I certainly did not fully connect with it until recently. As I look back, it was more of a subconscious protective guide for much of my life, or, more accurately, that is all I allowed it to be. I am still very much in the learning and growing phase of my awareness, and as I've learned to listen, I've begun to hear guidance for all areas of my life, not just the warnings and exclamations of danger! I'm talking everything from nudges to reach out to a specific person, to pay close attention to why a new person has shown up in my life, or to the out-of-the-blue need to check the whereabouts of one of my kids.

My guess is that most of us are similar in learning from mistakes or traumatic events in our lives. Learning to trust my intuition certainly took on a significant role in my life that way. When Connor first came out, it was the nudging of my intuition that pushed me to find information, ask questions, and keep digging for truth when it came to the questions around religion, what support he needed, what the coming out process was, etc. A few months later, the nudging was back, this time accompanied by a nagging feeling in my gut. Because this was uncomfortable, and I was already so overwhelmed, I ignored it. But intuition does not give up. It just grew more intense as each week passed. I knew it was trying to tell me something about Connor, but I was too afraid to listen—to do the work necessary to figure it out. And so, it continued, causing fatigue and significant weight loss. I was not yet aware of the concepts and practices of sitting through uncomfortable feelings with awareness or walking through challenges instead of trying to walk around them. My poor intuition was literally doing major work all on its own!

After months of the nagging feeling getting stronger and stronger, within the course of a week, I had flashing danger signs from so many different sources that I had to listen. As my world crashed around me and I faced the acute danger Connor was in, I allowed myself to open up to all the information my intuition had been trying to tell me.

I had taken Connor's phone from him after catching him sneaking out—again. I remember the fear gripping and clawing tighter with every passing moment. When I stumbled into my therapist's office that morning, the fears just gushed out of me like one unintelligible sound. Having known me long enough, she agreed that my intuition had been pointing me to what was about to be revealed.

I sat on my bathroom floor that night, shaking as I scrolled through Connor's open phone and just cried. Uncontrollable, heartbroken, terrified sobs came from deep within my soul. And I just let them come until they were all out. Not only was my intuition correct, but Connor was also in immediate danger, both physically from outside sources, as well as his own personal safety. As I quickly learned, the insidious world he was dipping his toe in, mixed with the already present layers of self-loathing and shame, made dying by suicide a very real possibility. One that we acted on immediately.

As I took deep breaths and centered myself that night, I was filled with intense gratitude for that beautiful voice within me. My intuition arguably shifted the course of numerous events for the good. I resolved to lean into my intuition from that moment on.

Learning to trust my intuition has been one more layer of my journey and education over the past few years. One that has brought joy and awareness, as well as warnings. Honing and listening to it have become a part of my daily practice.

Ways to Connect with Your Intuition

Thankfully, you can learn to listen to and trust your intuition in many ways. Meditation apps like Calm and Headspace have guided meditations specifically on honing your intuition. Meditation-specific blogs like *Tiny Buddha* and *Rebel Zen* are enlightening and fun ways to strengthen your meditation muscle. Here are a few more techniques I've used to help develop my intuition more fully.

- **Practice meditation.** One of the best ways to develop and connect with your intuition is through alpha state meditation. It is helpful for every aspect of your health and well-being. Deepak Chopra gives this scientific explanation behind why meditating to develop your intuition works: " . . . alpha [state] is the level that helps you learn, memorize, interact, and read the thoughts and emotions of others and yourself. The alpha state of the brain also relates to meditation. A daily meditation practice helps you control this alpha state, and therefore control the intuitive process."[1] So cool, right?!

- **Enlist all five of your senses.** Think about how you use your hearing, sight, taste, smell, and touch daily. What happens when you pay attention to the information each brings you? Becoming aware of the information each sense is taking in helps to develop your sixth sense, or intuition.
- **Allow your cognitive mind to rest.** When you tap into your creativity, you allow your intuition to speak up. Pay attention to your dreams too. Your cognitive mind is completely at rest then, which allows space for your intuition to develop. We only need to listen! We all dream; you just may not be accustomed to remembering what you dream. Try keeping a notebook by your bed and, upon waking, write anything you may remember. It takes a bit of practice and can give you genuine insight and connection to your intuition.
- **Pay attention to your gut.** Your intuition can speak through your physical body too. That's why the feeling it evokes can be referred to as a *gut feeling*. Pay attention to uncomfortable feelings that arise around decisions or specific situations. It may be your intuition trying to get your attention.
- **Unplug and get outside.** Being in nature, whether it is a walk on a quiet forest path or a barefoot stroll through your backyard, eliminates all distractions and allows you to connect with nature . . . and that beautiful inner voice.
- **Value your feelings.** We often place a lot of weight on the guidance of our rational mind, leaving our feelings as a distant second checkpoint. Our intuition shows up in our feelings. A wise friend once shared with me, "the mind is often bossy and harsh while the intuition speaks softly through your feelings."
- **Stay connected to your core values.** The mind can guide you away from your principles, but your intuition never will. Learn

the difference between how your body feels when you act in alignment with your values and how it feels when you do not.

- **Take a breath.** Try one of the breathing techniques that I shared in chapter two. Breathing techniques are great for honing our intuition because they allow us to disconnect from the endless noise in our minds and connect with our body and energy. In this elevated state of awareness, we can heal, grow, and evolve.

- **Create space for *being*.** When we make intentional time in our days to shift from busy to just being, it gives us the opportunity to be quiet, look inward, and listen. Remember the value of a pause? Taking that extra moment to shift out of your head into the present moment or what you feel allows for incredible expansion.

- **Live in the present and talk to your higher self.** Your higher self is your intuition! Practice creating a clear path of communication. Be aware of what you are communicating! Are you talking negatively to yourself or repeating fearful thoughts over and over? These things just clog up the communication channels, and you end up manifesting the very things you are most fearful of instead of what you most desire. Clear communication doesn't happen overnight. It takes patience and practice, but I promise, with conscious effort, it will become a powerful, effortless habit.

These strategies will create a solid foundation for you. Your intuition will guide you to your next step. (WINK, WINK)

Ponder and Reflect

Grab your journal and reflect! Don't overthink it. Just let your thoughts and feelings flow onto the page.

A parent's intuition is an incredible guide and shares valuable information if only one will listen.

- Take a moment and record how intuition has shown up in your life.
- Live in the present and talk to your higher self (your intuition!). Write about one thing you would like to tell yourself.
- When was the last time you were aware of your intuition? What did it tell you?
- Where do you feel your intuition? Close your eyes and picture it. Is it a pathway, a general place in your body (your torso), or someplace very specific (your stomach or your heart)?
- What clogs up your communication with your intuition?

CHAPTER FIFTEEN

Release Fear

Courage doesn't mean you don't get afraid. Courage
means you don't let fear stop you.

—BETHANY HAMILTON

I couldn't even begin to think clearly or rationally. As soon as Connor said those two words, "I'm gay," the fears and what-ifs began to explode like fireworks in my brain. Will his life be more challenging? Will he be bullied? Will he be targeted with cruelty and violence? What if people judge him? What if people judge us? Is he going to hell? As soon as I began to work through one question, ten more would explode.

During those first few weeks, I felt under constant attack, first mentally, and then the effects began to manifest physically: loss of appetite and weight, increased migraines, and restless sleep. Even though I'm a fighter, fighting this time required quadruple the energy. Supporting Connor, being a mom and all that entails, maintaining good energy in our house, working, and mentally shuffling through and attending to the never-ending list of to-dos had me stretched so thin and in so many directions. Fear was omnipresent; it affected me mentally, physically, and emotionally.

Fear

It's a small word that can wreak complete havoc in our lives. It can cause us to freeze. It can cause us to lash out in ugly or hateful ways. It can cause us to shy away from our dreams. It can deter us from listening to our intuition. Fear is the absence of love.

I argue that fear may be one of the most insidious emotions humans experience. It is snakelike in its ability to stealthily weave itself throughout the fabric of our days and nights, not becoming evident until we are frozen, panic-stricken, overwhelmed, or irrationally lashing out. Most of us do not recognize the subtle power fear has over every aspect of our lives until we shine a big spotlight on it.

There is a difference between fear and anxiety, even though they often travel together. Fear is typically connected to something specific and often occurs in the moment. Anxiety is more ambiguous and often tags along as a subtle, low-level stressor that can't really be named or pointed to directly. Both fear and anxiety trigger your body's fight-or-flight response. They also share similar physical sensations, like a racing heart, muscle tension, a cold chill, and an increased breathing rate.

Knowing the difference between the two is helpful as we learn to evict fear. Like everything else, time and practice are involved in this process, but the good news is that there are strategies, the most simple being: BE AWARE!

Awareness

Awareness and being present pretty much go hand in hand. When you pull yourself out of your thoughts and focus on this present moment, fear cannot take hold. You have eliminated the what-if thoughts that fear loves to cling to.

So, let's name some of those fears. I want you to take a moment to add to the list all your fears about your child being LGBTQ+. Remember, being a fear *doesn't* make them true or accurate.

- They will be bullied
- Their life will be harder

- We can't control what they will find on apps and the internet
- STDs, especially HIV
- Their safety
- Finding true friends and true love

Ponder and Reflect

Grab your journal and make a list of your fears or concerns. (I know it's right in the middle of the chapter—but this is important!)

. . . . .

Once you are in a place of awareness, I want you to try at least one of the following strategies:

- **Name it to tame it.** Take your list from above, and next to each one, write out the worst-case scenario. Write how likely it is to happen (very likely/ likely/ somewhat likely/ slightly likely/ not at all likely). This brings clarity to each fear; it pulls it out of the shadows and stops it from snaking through your life.
- **Share it out loud with someone you trust.** Just the act of saying out loud and processing through what the fear is, why it is, and what the potential outcomes may be will help you diffuse its power and hold on you. This can also help you shift perspective. Is there a positive way to look at this fear?
- **Question what the fear is based on.** Is that information accurate? Where did the information come from? Make a list of evidence and counter-evidence. You need to be a detective here and use the logical side of your brain. You may need to walk away and come back to this step after a few hours or even a few days. That space will allow you to peel back the layers.
- **Breathe.** The power of a deep, intentional breath cannot be overstated. Deep, mindful breathing activates your body's

parasympathetic nervous system, which, in simple terms, deactivates your body's stress response. It helps to ground you, calm you, and bring you back into the present moment.

- **Embrace it!** Remember when I talked about facing fear head-on, saying, "I see you fear. I know you are trying to protect me, but I've got this!" Saying this out loud sends a powerful message to your entire mental, physical, and spiritual system and, in doing so, empowers you to continue on this path of learning, healing, and growing.

Facing our fears is HARD, but something extraordinary happens when we do. Their power over us begins to diminish. We feel frozen and overwhelmed less often. The more awareness we practice, the better we become at stopping fear at the door.

Of course, fear will never go away entirely. Our body and mind responding with fear to actual threats is necessary for our survival. But most fears do not fit in that category, and I have learned in the past few years that when fear presents itself in specific ways, it is a sign that I need to push through it. We can learn to manipulate fear to help us grow and evolve!

As I was in my process, I became relentless about figuring out the *what*, *where*, *why*, and *how*, as in:

- *What* information, strategies, tips, and practices will help me overcome my fears?
- *Where* can I find accurate information and support?
- *Why* is there so much hate (a form of fear) directed toward the LGBTQ+ community?
- *How* can I be a good ally and advocate?

This relentlessness helped me discover some fascinating facts. For example, wanting to understand *why* there is so much hate directed toward the LGBTQ+ community, I learned that while Sigmund Freud is remembered and referenced for his work on the psychology of sexuality, I had no idea he was ground zero for what is now widely recognized to be scientifically inaccurate assumptions about homosexuality. He *guessed* that being homosexual related to how a child was socialized, an assumption that those wishing to spread fear have taken out of the context of Freud's research and doubled down on for over a century.[1]

These false claims have steeped themselves in the fabric of our culture, where it is still believed by some that overbearing parents and social contact with those in the LGBTQ+ community can cause one to be gay (or bi or trans, etc.). These beliefs have no scientific backing. And they are a direct cause of fear and misinformation that is layered and passed from generation to generation.

There is good news in all of this, however. Peer-reviewed research has ruled out socialization, parental influence, and choice as a cause of sexual orientation.[2] Science. Facts. Knowing and sharing the truth about this and so many other false beliefs about LGBTQ+ people help demolish fear. (If you are curious about this specific research, as well as other resources, take a look at the resource section in the back of the book.)

Ponder and Reflect

Grab your journal and reflect! Don't overthink it. Just let your thoughts and feelings flow onto the page.

- Set a timer and write every fear you can imagine.
- Write where you think they stem from, why they no longer serve you, and set them free.
- Listen to Episode 16 of *Just Breathe: Parenting Your LGBTQ Teen*, "When It Feels Scary."[3]
- Try my meditation on fear[4] for extra support.

Action Steps for Pillar Three: Empower

- Ally/Advocate
    - » In what ways can you be an advocate for your child and an ally for the LGBTQ+ community?
    - » How can you teach allyship to others?
- Communicate: Practice the VAST technique.
    - » Validate
    - » Ask
    - » See them
    - » Talk
- Intuition: How in tune are you with your intuition? Commit to trying at least three of the following techniques for honing your intuition.
    - » meditate
    - » enlist all five senses
    - » allow your cognitive mind to rest
    - » discover where you feel intuition in your body
    - » unplug and get outside
    - » value your feelings
    - » stay connected to your core values
    - » breathwork
    - » create space for being
    - » live in the present and talk to your higher self
- Fear: Name it to tame it! Awareness and knowledge are two keys to banishing fear. Write down one way you will actively confront your fears. Every time you do this, it will increase your feeling of empowerment. Teach this to your kids as well.
- Check in with yourself and look ahead.

- Where are you right now? Record your goals.
  - » One-week goal
  - » One-month goal
  - » One-year goal

· · · · ·

This is not a race . . . there is no deadline. Be gentle with yourself and with your child as you learn to become empowered and empower others. And remember . . . you are not alone!

Pillar Four: Love

*T*here's a reason that the love pillar is last. Everything we've learned through the first three pillars—embracing our child and their sexual orientation and/or gender identity, educating ourselves in many different ways, and empowering ourselves and our children—builds the foundation and understanding of unconditional love. While love is woven into each chapter, in this pillar, we'll focus on loving yourself, loving your child, and doing our very best to share that love unconditionally. If there is only one thing that you take away from this book, let it be this: *Love your child unconditionally for who they are right now in this moment in time. See them, hear them, love them.*

CHAPTER SIXTEEN

Love Yourself

Just be yourself. Let people see the real,
imperfect, flawed, quirky, weird, beautiful,
magical person that you are.

—MANDY HALE

We all know we should love who we are—ALL of who we are.
We truly cannot be effective in loving our children, or anyone
else for that matter, until we fully love ourselves—all of the
beauty, all of the flaws, and everything in between. Some days it's easy,
and others, not so much! I previously shared the basics of self-compassion—what it is and why it is important. Self-compassion is a big
component of loving one's self.

Loving who you are allows you to show up in the world and with
your child as the very best version of yourself. Accepting and embracing that you are human does a couple of really cool things:

- It allows you to move through your days more fluidly. As you
  stop beating yourself up for every mistake and flaw and begin
  to see those mistakes and flaws as teachers and guides, your
  desire for perfection will diminish drastically, as will your
  self-criticism and stress!

- It helps you model grace for your kids. When our kids see us
  owning and allowing our mistakes or missteps to be teachers,
  they soak that in! In permitting ourselves to be human, we give

that gift to our kids as well. Practice sharing your mistakes and the lessons you've learned out loud. It may feel a bit messy at first, and that's okay! The whole idea is to model ways that you love and accept yourself for all of your pieces so that your kids can learn to do the same.

According to Deborah Khoshaba from *Psychology Today*, "Self-love is not simply a state of feeling good. It is a state of appreciation for oneself that grows from actions that support our physical, psychological, and spiritual growth. Self-love is dynamic; it grows through actions that mature us."[1] So, how can we develop a deep love of self? Like so many other things I am sharing with you, we develop a love of self through practice and awareness. This is something that I work on daily. Some days it comes easier than others, but I have found that focusing on at least one of the following tips every day is super helpful, even on the hard days. Find your favorites and build a ritual.

These are great tips to share with all your kids, especially your LGBTQ+ kiddo. The opposite of self-love, self-loathing, is a pervasive and potentially dangerous part of the coming out process, so learning self-compassion early on will be soothing, empowering, and even life-saving.

Physical Growth

There is something very calming about having a list of possible strategies or tools on this journey of self-discovery, self-love, and potential exponential growth. I believe we all want to continue growing; it's the *how* that can really stump us. So, once again, I'm offering a few ideas that will help kick-start your list. Physical growth includes good self-care, finding a creative outlet, and cleaning out.

PRACTICE GOOD SELF-CARE: 4 MAIN COMPONENTS

1. **Move** that beautiful body every day! Do what feels good and gets your blood pumping.

2. **Nourish** your body with foods that help this extraordinary, complex machine work optimally for you! I am all about moderation, not deprivation. Chocolate, caffeine, the occasional cocktail—whatever your guilty culinary pleasures are—indulge every once in a while. Just make sure they are the exception and not the rule.

3. **Sleep**, yep, I'm mentioning this again because it is that important. Every facet of your life will work better and move more smoothly when you get restful, restorative sleep. There are many helpful apps, such as ShutEye and Sleep Cycle. The bottom line is to make sleep a priority.

4. **Healthy intimacy**–I know, whoa, treading a boundary here! Study after study has shown that a healthy, physical connection with your spouse or partner deepens love and appreciation for yourself, as well as your loved one—double bonus here!

FIND YOUR CREATIVE OUTLET

What activities turn off that inner critic and allow you to express yourself? Painting? Music? Gardening? Writing? Appreciating and practicing the ways in which you are creative and expressive support your physical growth and, thus, the love of self.

CLEAN OUT!

You may laugh at first at this one, but think about it for a minute—when you clear out or organize something in your physical space, it has a domino effect in all other areas, right? Your mind feels clearer, you have increased energy, and you feel more connected to yourself, your purpose, and those around you. Often, when I have a ton on my plate, I choose one small thing to clean or organize: a shelf in the fridge, my desk, or a load of laundry. Something in the act of cleaning or organizing calms that ever-swirling to-do list and allows me to focus on the most critical task at that moment.

Psychological Growth: 9 Positive Actions

Let's move from taking care of our physical or external world to focusing on our psychological or internal world. The following eight actions support your growth. Pick one or two at a time and see what resonates with you.

1. **Practice mindfulness.** Become more aware of what YOU think, feel, and want, and learn to act on that. This builds self-love. Making time to calm your mind every day will build this awareness. Use your breathing exercises from chapter two.

2. **Integrate healthy social interaction.** Humans are social beings. Build a community of your people, those who love and support you, and vice versa.

3. **Set boundaries.** Boundaries are essential when it comes to self-love because they send a message of self-respect to the brain and psyche. Self-respect is a form of self-love.

4. **Use positive affirmations and positive self-talk.** I know affirmations and self-talk can feel goofy or awkward. I was resistant until I started with a short list of affirmations that I wrote on my bathroom mirror. Try writing your own affirmations in a place where you will see them every day. Repeat over and over each morning and evening, perhaps as you brush your teeth. You will be amazed at what can happen. Not only will it pull you out of spinning thoughts and negative self-talk that don't serve you, but it will also shift your mood and daily outlook. In addition to the affirmations in my bathroom, I also have a deck of affirmation cards in my office that I pull from every day!

5. **Stop the comparisons.** You are beautifully, uniquely, fabulously YOU! There is no other human on this planet like you. Embrace and love who you are, flaws and all. One of my favorite authors, Anne Lamont, said, "Never compare your insides to someone else's outsides." These are wise words to live by.

6. **Incorporate the concept of *and*.** We are conditioned to think that most thoughts or choices are either/or. However, when you stop to think about it, many statements, feelings, and beliefs can be *and* instead of *either/or* and, in fact, feel so much better when we word them that way. Another way to think about

using *and* is to swap out or reverse a *but* and use *and* instead. For example, swap out "I love my kids, BUT sometimes they drive me nuts," for "I love my kids AND sometimes they drive me nuts." Think, "My work is so fulfilling, AND sometimes it is exhausting," instead of, "My work is so fulfilling, BUT sometimes it is exhausting." Try one of your own. It really is a magical mental shift.

7. **Learn to say "No."** This doesn't make you a bad person; it makes you a wise, grounded, connected, and aware person. Sit with that and let it soak in. Here are some hints for saying no:
   » Giving people words, not excuses, can be powerful. One of these words can simply be *no*.
   » If *no* is the first word that comes to mind when someone asks you to do something that just doesn't feel aligned with you, just say it. You are responsible for you, not another's need or response.
   » Phrases like, "No, that doesn't work for me," or "No, not right now," allow for space and time to consider your answer.

8. **Let go.** Let go of past trauma, wounds, pain, anger, and disappointments. This is hard and requires conscious effort and perhaps even professional support. When we hold on to the past, it weighs us down psychologically, which also spills over onto our physical and spiritual health. I know holding on may seem initially protective, but in the long run, it just creates blocks for us—blocks to living our beautiful, authentic life and blocks to self-acceptance and self-love.

9. **Make a running "I'm awesome" list.** What do you most love about yourself? Keep a list. Add one thing to it every day. Read it when you wake up in the morning and before you go to bed at night.

Spiritual Growth: 5 Essential Practices

Spiritual growth is the path to deepen your love of self. Remember, spirituality is not synonymous with religion. Some of you may find spiritual peace in your house of worship, while others may find it in nature or on your yoga mat. There is no one right way to grow spiritually. Listen to your heart and your intuition. Neither will steer you wrong. Allow the following practices to support you, and add to them as you come up with more.

1. **Forgive yourself.** Allow yourself to be human. We are our own biggest critics, right? Each of us must find our unique sweet spot in the middle of owning our mistakes and punishing ourselves for them. Let's all try more learning and growing, less self-critique, more acceptance of our humanity, and fewer expectations of perfection.

2. **Treat others with love and respect.** Yes, the golden rule. I also like to think of it as karma, or what you put out into the world, you will get back. And, let's face it, it always feels better to treat others with love and respect. The more you do this, the stronger and deeper your self-love will grow. Don't worry about whether others reflect love and respect back to you—that would be nice, but their response is their problem, not yours.

3. **Practice daily gratitude.** This is one of my favorite ways to lean into love—for myself, my kids, my husband, and for everything and everyone in my environment, near and far. Gratitude could be a full book, but it is an item on a list for now. We often overthink what gratitude should be or how we should express it. The most important thing is to simply recognize and express it. Take that big, beautiful breath, and quiet your mind. What comes up for you? Write that down. Connect with your passion and your purpose. Be detailed about your physical and mental health. There is no right way to express and feel gratitude. It can be in a journal or just on a Post-it note. It can be the last thing you do every night as you drift off to sleep or the first thing you do in the precious quiet of the morning.

4. **Explore your faith.** What actions can you take that will help you grow spiritually? What does faith look like for you right now? Would you like for it to look any different? Remember, religion and faith are two separate things. Your spiritual growth is a crucial component of self-acceptance and self-love.

5. **Lean into your intuition.** As we learned in pillar three, when we lean into instead of questioning our intuition, our sense of empowerment deepens and allows us to radiate it to others. Leaning into our intuition applies to self-love and love as well! Learning how to listen to that beautiful inner wisdom builds trust. Trusting ourselves is a form of love. The more we trust our inner voice, the deeper our spiritual connection will be. Isn't it cool how these are all interconnected?!

Reflect and allow space and time to explore how you can incorporate the ideas from above that resonate most with you. Start with one form of growth—physical, psychological, or spiritual—and try at least one strategy that helps you deepen your love for yourself. These exercises may feel weird at first. It's okay. You are learning to see, value, and fully love the most important human being: YOU! Live intentionally, follow your passion, and find your happy place.

Ponder and Reflect

Grab your journal and reflect! Don't overthink it. Just let your thoughts and feelings flow onto the page.

- What do you NEED to take care of yourself to show yourself some love?
- What actions or strategies will you try to help you deepen your love for yourself?
- Where might you benefit from decluttering or mental shifts, including eliminating toxic relationships, saying "No," and letting go?
- Incorporate the concept of *and*, which is essentially reversing a *but* statement. For example, "I love my children, AND sometimes they drive me nuts." Try writing a few of your own *and* statements.
- Next time you catch yourself saying *but* in a sentence, try switching it to *and* and see how it shifts the meaning of the sentence for you.

CHAPTER SEVENTEEN

Love Your Child

Children need at least one person in their life that
thinks the sun rises and sets on them, who delights in
their existence, and loves them unconditionally.

—PAMELA LEO

When you first picked up this book, you may have thought,
"Why do I need a chapter on how to love my child? I know this
already!" But hopefully, after reading the previous chapter on
loving yourself, you realize that there are many nuances to this topic
and perhaps different ways to show, feel, and communicate love to and
for our children. It may even bring up the deeper question of *why* is it
important that our children feel and know they are loved.

I have found it to be very useful to have options to choose from:
ideas, tools, and strategies that are proven, even if anecdotally. That's
what I'd like to offer you now—a plethora of choices. After all, what
works for one teen may not work as well for another.

Speak Your Kids' Love Language

Understanding love languages—your children's, your partner's,
and your own—was quite popular a few years ago. You can take the
details of the concept for whatever they're worth to you; however, the
general idea is a good one to add to your toolbox.

Gary Chapman authored the series of love language books, which are written around the concept of five love languages: *words of affirmation, physical touch, quality time, acts of service,* and *gifts.*[1]

What do these love languages look like in action?

Use words of affirmation whenever you notice something they do well or acknowledge when they have completed a task you know was stressful. Be specific and sincere.

Physical touch can be as simple as making up a cool "secret" handshake with one of your kids! Sharing love with touch can also be sensory-oriented—buy your teen a soft blanket or fluffy pillow if this is something that soothes them.

Quality time simply means being present. Don't overthink this. Cook or bake together, take a drive or walk to their favorite coffee shop, or watch a movie together—the less complicated, the better.

The key to acts of service is performing the service without expecting anything in return. Over time, our children pick up on these behaviors and model them in their own way. Here are a few ideas: when they are stressed or overwhelmed, help with tasks to relieve pressure, make their favorite meal, or pick up a few of their favorite items when you are shopping.

My husband loves to give gifts to express his love. Whether it is a cool pair of shoes for one of us or a favorite treat, he is delighted to give it as his way of saying, "I saw this today and thought of you." If gifts are your teen's love language, give a gift that shows you know them and respect who they are or recognize their dreams for the present and future. Neither the size nor the expense matters; when you give from the heart with the intent of strengthening your connection with your child, all materialism fades away.

As one whose primary love language is physical touch, I must actively remind myself that even though I want to express my love by hugging my kids, none of their primary love languages is physical touch, so that is NOT an effective way to communicate. In fact, it is sometimes seen as boundary hopping or just plain irritating. Learning to express, offer, and communicate love in the way each of my kids (and my husband!) most resonate with has been a huge energy-shifter for us.

Talk to Our Kids So They Feel Loved

From the moment these precious little humans arrive into our lives, it is easy to feel overwhelmed as a parent. Our responsibility is to love them, provide for their basic needs, keep them safe, and guide them as they grow. As we take into consideration how we approach parenting, the physical environment in which we are raising our children, and, perhaps most importantly, who our children are, we begin to realize the endless options available.

Accept ahead of time that you will make mistakes. Take a breath. Our overarching goals are to raise children who are resilient, compassionate, and capable adults. Give yourself grace as you learn.

Here are three conversations you can have with your children that will not only communicate your unconditional love for them but will also teach them how to love themselves and others. These conversations can start when they are very young, and you can add depth and detail as they get older.

- **Let them know they are loved for who they are right now and who they will become in the future.** Make it clear that these are separate. Doing this creates trust in you and your relationship. At age five, this conversation may be "Last year, you loved digging in the sand at the beach, and this year, you are building cool sand mounds; it is so much fun for me to watch as what you like to do changes!" At age fifteen, this conversation may be "Thank you for sharing with me who you have a crush on; I love you no matter who you love." In addition to trust, this helps your child build high self-esteem and strong social skills.
- **Let them know their home is a safe place to share their feelings.** Encourage them to give words to the emotions they feel on the inside. When you begin this when they are young, you help them develop a higher emotional intelligence, also known as EQ. One way to develop EQ is by teaching the vocabulary around feelings and giving them the space to ask questions and connect with whatever emotion they have.

Another technique that works no matter their age is reflecting the emotion or the behavior you are seeing and following up with a question. One example that has worked for me and many of my clients is an approach for a quiet teen. You can say, "Hey, you were pretty quiet at the dinner table tonight. I wonder if you are tired or if you have a lot of thoughts rolling around in your head or feelings in your body that you might want to just get out." Even if they default to being tired, you let them know that you see them, that you are available in a non-invasive way, and you shared an important distinction between thoughts and feelings.

- **Let them know that everyone is learning and everyone makes mistakes—no matter how old they are!** By imparting this message over and over throughout childhood, adolescence, and young adulthood, you help shape how your children learn. Instead of learning to be critical of themselves when they make a mistake or when something is hard, they learn problem-solving skills, perseverance, and patience.[2]

Show Our Kids They Are Loved

Did you know that showing our kids how much we love them is one of the most powerful and protective things we can do? But what does that mean, and how do we do it? Showing is a pretty broad term, after all.

As it turns out, there are several key factors that help us to show our love and create a beautiful, protective bubble around them.

- **Show warmth and support.** Think of your favorite ways to show warmth and support to your kids. A hug or an arm around their shoulder? What about listening to their very detailed story, even when you can barely keep your eyes open late at night? How about going with your child to a pride event or helping them find an LGBTQ+ peer group? It can be as simple as a wink or a shared smile and knowing glance!
- **Set clear limits and boundaries.** Having clear limits and boundaries is a powerful way to show our love. Not only are

limits and boundaries protective, but they also create a sense of safety and stability for our kids. Limits and boundaries may not be the most exciting way to show love, but having them in place communicates love on a much deeper level.

- **Be flexible.** At first glance, flexibility may not make sense. But think of it as the opposite of rigidity. When we can show our kids that we are flexible in our thinking (willing to learn) and flexible in our approach to situations (willing to grow), it is one of the most fulfilling ways to show our love to and for our children.
- **Give them space to make mistakes.** This builds on the idea that everyone makes mistakes one important step further. We can explain and give examples, but then we have to step back. As they make mistakes, we *show* acceptance and give them room to grow and have their own experiences. This can be easier said than done. It is uncomfortable to see our kids struggle or fail. It was a game changer for me to envision myself as the safety net instead of the interference! That being said, there will be times when you will need to interfere for safety reasons, whether it is physical or mental safety. You know your kid. Start with a little space for small failures. As you get more comfortable with your role of safety net and your child realizes you will always be there to support them, the trust grows, which in turn allows for more and more space.

Model these factors. It doesn't matter how many times you say, "Do as I say, not as I do." They will almost always do as you do. Modeling warmth and support, boundary setting, flexibility, and patience with mistakes all require a level of conscious parenting that may be difficult at first. It's okay. Remember, you are human, and you may be learning one or two of these for the first time yourself. Pick one and practice. Share your process with your kids. They will love learning alongside you!

Bottomline, express love verbally and non-verbally.[3] The value of a verbal "I love you" is quite underrated. Say it. A lot. Especially as your kids enter their teen years. It may seem like they want nothing to do with you, and they may even roll their eyes or shrug it off when you tell them but know that you are reinforcing that solid base for them, and they secretly soak it in. Consider the non-verbal ways you express love or any other emotion as well. Be aware of how these non-verbal expressions are being received by your teen. Try different ways to express love verbally and non-verbally. You will find one that hits a sweet spot with your child, and that will be a game-changer!

Ponder and Reflect

Grab your journal and reflect! Don't overthink it. Just let your thoughts and feelings flow onto the page.

It is particularly important for our LGBTQ+ kids to know they are loved.

- How can we talk to them and show them they are loved?
- What expressions can you think of that are specific to your LGBTQ+ child?
- What expressions can you think of that are specific to your other children?

CHAPTER EIGHTEEN

Love Unconditionally

The depth of the love parents have for their children
cannot be measured. It is like no other relationship. It
exceeds concern for life itself. The love of a parent for a
child is continuous and transcends heartbreak
and disappointment.

—JAMES E. FAUST

nderstanding unconditional love is one of those things that
most of us think we inherently know, but it can get easily
mucked up by our subconscious and by what we were taught or
experienced as children or young adults. So what is unconditional love,
and more importantly, how do we give it or show it?

My favorite explanation of this surprisingly complicated concept is
from the website MindBodyGreen:

> The term unconditional love does not mean love without lim-
> its or bounds. It means, "I offer you my love freely without
> condition." This means that when we offer our love, we offer it
> without expectation of repayment. It is important to offer this
> type of unconditional love in our relationships. Otherwise, we
> are offering love with "strings attached." This creates power
> and control imbalances. Unconditional love means loving
> someone through hardships, mistakes, and frustrations.[1]

I think that last sentence bears repeating for all of us as we parent our teenagers: "Unconditional love means loving someone through hardships, mistakes, and frustrations." I actually want to add one more here: Unconditional love means loving someone *without* qualifications such as, "I love you, but . . . ." It is love without a list of boxes to check.

Another way to think of unconditional love, and one that especially resonates with our LGBTQ+ teenagers, is "You are my child; I will never reject you." Pause with that for a moment and let it sink in. Every tool and strategy I've shared with you has been a building block toward this one statement of unconditional love.

The importance of how we choose our words cannot be overstated. We are going to get angry and frustrated. That is just a human part of parenting teenagers. Instead of "I'm mad at you," try "I love you, but I am disappointed in your actions" or "I don't like this behavior." Saying "I'm mad at you" is too general and just creates noise in their brains. Depending on where they are in their coming out process or generally in their mental health development, "I'm mad at you" can be translated a million different ways. When we are specific and remind them first that we love them and nothing can change that love—and then focus on an action or behavior, they can digest that and work on it, feeling secure in your love.

Unconditional love is the ultimate foundation AND encapsulation of a deep connection with not only your LGBTQ+ teen, but also your other children and spouse or partner as well! It is complete acceptance of another or by another as a whole, perfectly imperfect human being.

Unconditional love tends to be one phrase that gets used without proper understanding of its meaning. To allow that love to come from the heart, not the mind—love that is not based on actions or behaviors, but just is—this is unconditional love. This is how we're meant to love our kids. It is just part of the parenting deal. Genuinely unconditional love becomes evident when a crisis, struggle, or other challenging situation arises, for example, when your child comes out to you or expresses thoughts, ideas, or values that are different from yours. What we do, say, and feel in these moments can hinder or build relationships with our children.

To be clear, I do not believe this means we don't ever get to be angry or frustrated with behaviors or that we can't set boundaries or be human. This is another excellent example of *and*—your love for your child can be without conditions, *and* you can set rules for behavior expectations. It can be both. In fact, practicing unconditional love makes it a bit easier for us to set boundaries and for our children to follow set rules. It also allows everyone involved to be human and know that we are still loved. How cool is that?

Unconditional love embraces all of the beauty and the messiness of the LGBTQ+ coming out process and allows you to authentically move forward with awareness and genuine acceptance. I encourage you to marinate in all you have learned and continue doing the growth work needed to really see your child and understand all that they need.

Ponder and Reflect

Grab your journal and reflect! Don't overthink it. Just let your thoughts and feelings flow onto the page.

- What does unconditional love mean to you?
- Do you have conditions around your love? If so, journal ideas for letting those conditions go.

Focus on the following actions in each conversation with your teen:

- See who they are right now, at this moment in time.
- Authentically empower them.
- Sincerely encourage them.

Think of how you show your love best.

- What are ways that you express unconditional love?
- Do you want to make any shifts in your life around unconditional love? If so, where?

Action Steps for Pillar Four: Love

Take some time to journal your thoughts on the following:

- What is one tool or strategy you plan on trying to deepen your self-love and self-compassion?
- What is your child's love language? What is one way you can communicate with them in their love language?
- Has your understanding of unconditional love changed? If so, in what way?
- Write your personal definition of unconditional love.
- Check in with yourself and look ahead.
- Where are you right now? Record your goals.
    » One-week goal
    » One-month goal
    » One-year goal

. . . . .

This is not a race . . . there is no deadline. Be gentle with yourself and with your child. Most of all, love them for who they are, right now, in this moment in time. And remember . . . you are not alone!

CHAPTER NINETEEN

The Four Pillars in Action

Embrace Educate Empower Love

This chapter is where all of the pillars come together, and you get to have a bit of fun!

Just like naming your fears can calm you and bring clarity, having a plan or a blueprint can empower you. One of the beautiful things about the pillars is that they are not a one-size-fits-all solution. They can be molded and tweaked to support you and your family where you are now and then molded and tweaked to support you where you are a year or ten years from now!

In these final pages, I am going to share a simple diagram of the pillars, as well as a few examples of the pillars in action. Use the diagram on the following page to put together all the ideas we've talked about, and begin to embrace the beauty as well as the messiness of this process. If something doesn't work, know that you are still learning. Be compassionate with yourself and your teen. They are watching and learning from you!

EMBRACE

- Ensure your teen knows you see them, love them, and have their back
- Open the door of communication
- Allow vulnerability and evolution

EDUCATE AND UNLEARN BIAS

- Learn about the coming out process for your kid and for you
- Reach out for support
- Be aware of substance abuse and mental health

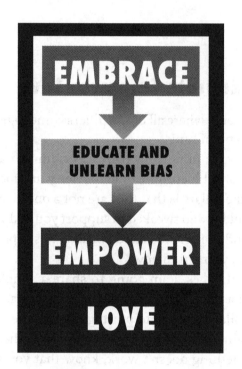

EMPOWER

- Create unapologetic boundaries
- Become an advocate and ally
- Connect with your intuition
- Let go of fear

LOVE

- Love yourself and allow for personal growth
- Love your child for who they are right now
- Express unconditional love verbally and nonverbally

Let's look at how a few principles from the pillars of embrace, educate and unlearn bias, empower, and love help families.

I met Dan and Eileen about six months after their fifteen-year-old daughter, Amelia, had come out to them as a lesbian. (All names are changed for privacy.) Dan and Eileen were affirming and supportive and knew that Amelia was struggling but didn't know how to help her. It took a few weeks of unraveling and processing to discover that she was self-harming. Self-harm can be difficult to detect, especially if our kids do not want us to know. Remember what you learned in chapter thirteen. Do not beat yourself up for not figuring it out right away!

Using the pillars helped Dan and Eileen slow down and take a breath. Even though they beautifully embraced Amelia when she came out, they still retraced those steps to make sure she knew she was loved and that they were going to be with her every step of her process.

Dan and Eileen really put the VAST communication technique to the test one afternoon as they were getting ready to go to a family event. They later recalled to me that they realized that Amelia was really struggling on that particular day, but they also needed to get out the door. So, in an effort to motivate her and ease the discomfort of the moment, they used statements that included phrases such as, "You've got so much potential to be . . ." and "Let's focus on the future and not how difficult it is now," and then Amelia burst out, "Don't you care about who I am right now?!" They all stopped and stared at each other, feeling the intense magnitude of the statement. She didn't need to be motivated, fixed, or tiptoed around. She needed to be seen.

Dan and Eileen admitted they really didn't understand what being seen meant before this moment, but this interaction made it crystal clear. They were able to back up, validate her request, and acknowledge the clarity it brought for them. In turn, Amelia began to share some of her fears and inner process. Feeling seen, heard, and validated helped her feel safe and allowed her to slowly lower the walls she had built up around her. Shifting from future focus to present focus took so much pressure off who she thought her parents wanted her to be and allowed her to let her authentic self shine through.

With a combined use of techniques and professional support, this family was able to get to the root of the self-harm, and Amelia learned and began practicing tools to help her heal, as well as move forward through her coming out process in a healthy way.

This next story is a lovely example of using elements of the pillars to puzzle through one situation over the course of a few hours. It begins with a son asking if he could bring his friend Sarah (her name has been changed to respect her privacy) with the family to see a play. Once the family was seated for the play, the mom spent the first act feeling perplexed because Sarah was so familiar to her. It finally dawned on her that Sarah was her son's friend whom she first knew as Brian (again, name has been changed for privacy), who had transitioned.

On the drive home from the play, this mother voiced her realization with love and grace . . . and a little laughter about her confusion. Both her son and Sarah expressed their gratitude for the way she handled the evening. As she shared the story with me later, she expressed the surprise she felt in the moment, but also her awareness that love and acceptance transcend any opinion or thought of how the situation could have been handled.

Because this mom already had elements of the educate pillar, she was able to employ an embrace of the situation, empowerment of herself and of the kids, and lots of love right in the moment when it was needed.

The last illustration of the pillars at work is part of the journey of a client. When we first met, her son was out as gay to only her and two close friends. She completely embraced him and had already done a lot of the work from pillar one, embrace, on her own. She was now seeking education and empowerment.

She had so many questions, such as, "What is the difference between gay and bisexual?" "My son is really struggling with depression and anxiety—why is that, and how can I support him?" "There are so many words I don't understand. I want to learn, and I want to know how to ask questions when I don't understand." "How do I help him navigate dating—I have no idea how to guide him or what advice to give!"

Over the course of a few weeks, several hours together, and many hours of work on her own, not only did she feel better informed, but she also felt validated and strengthened so that she could more fully understand and empower her son. Knowing the answers to her above questions, as well as ones pertaining to dating and the online world, helped her navigate conversations with her son, as well as guide him on his journey so that he could avoid some common pitfalls surrounding dating.

As you can see, the strategies, techniques, and lessons from each pillar can be used in many ways to support you and your child on this journey. They can be molded to fit your unique situation and tweaked to work for parent and child alike. You need only an open mind, a little creativity, and perhaps a dash of patience as you find what works for you. Use the knowledge you have accumulated as you've read and researched as well as the ideas and personal discoveries in your journal to help create a personalized blueprint for your family. Check in with the goals you made in the action steps sections for each pillar and continue to set new goals as you learn together with your family. Oh yeah, and remember—unconditional love embraces all the beauty and the messiness of parenting your LGBTQ+ teen!

A life journey is a series of intentional steps
guided by courage, wisdom, planning, patience,
love, and enthusiasm.

—HEATHER HESTER

Congratulations! You have completed the book. You have taken an enormous step in your personal growth and the deepening of the relationships with all of your children, especially your LGBTQ+ child. This is the first step forward in many to come. You have met fear head-on and said, "No, thank you, I've got this!"

I encourage you to continue your reflective exploration; take what resonates and nourishes you as a human being. The four pillars—Embrace, Educate and Unlearn Bias, Empower, and Love—are for anyone who knows and loves an LGBTQ+ kid. The transformations within the pillars and within you can affect change within your family, your community, and, ultimately, the world. I invite you to join me to help spread education and love to every corner of the world.

It has been an honor and privilege to be part of your journey. One day at a time. One small shift, one small action, one small effort.

xo,
Heather

Keep Learning!

Further Reading

BOOKS

- *Is It a Choice? Answers to the Most Frequently Asked Questions About Gay & Lesbian People* by Eric Marcus
- *Mom, I'm Gay: Loving Your LGBTQ Child Without Sacrificing Your Faith* by Susan Cottrell
- *The Savvy Ally: A Guide for Becoming a Skilled LGBTQ+ Advocate* by Jeannie Gainsburg
- *This Is a Book for Parents of Gay Kids: A Question & Answer Guide to Everyday Life This Is a Book for Parents of Gay Kids* by Dannielle Owens-Reid and Kristin Russo
- *Raising LGBTQ Allies: A Parent's Guide to Changing the Messages from the Playground* by Chris Tompkins

WEBSITES

- ACLU, www.aclu.org
- Chrysalis Mama, https://chrysalismama.com/resources
- GLAAD, https://glaad.org
- GLSEN, https://www.glsen.org
- Human Rights Campaign, www.hrc.org
- IGLYO, https://www.iglyo.com/
- It Gets Better Project, https://itgetsbetter.org
- Mental Health Awareness Education, https://mentalhealthawarenesseducation.com/
- PFLAG, www.pflag.org

- Planned Parenthood,
  https://www.plannedparenthood.org/learn
- Outright International, https://outrightinternational.org/
- Rainbow Railroad, https://www.rainbowrailroad.org/
- The Trevor Project, http://www.thetrevorproject.org
- TrevorSpace, https://www.trevorspace.org

Podcasts

- *Just Breathe: Parenting Your LGBTQ Teen*, https://open.spotify.
  com/show/68VAPuAB78DeeUV2SvM9mP?si=68e2e56263d5453f
  - » "Hey Parents, This is What Your Teen Wants You to Know!" (Episode 7)
  - » "Connor Shares His Story" (Episodes 21-23)
- *Let's Talk All Things LGBTQ+*, https://open.spotify.com/
  show/6aGdVTUcLoM8HPPSqZRQr2?si=4a513b1ce4a44cbb
- *Life (UN)Closeted*, https://open.spotify.com/show/
  6LXns3mJ2XfgR8fAreTsSQ
- *We Can Do Hard Things*, https://open.spotify.com/show/
  oeFL5HJejQHZrdgAFdPnOm?si=c562e47ba4254136

Apps

- Calm
- Headspace
- HidrateSpark
- iBreathe
- Paced Breathing
- The Breathing App
- The Tapping Solution
- Shut Eye
- Sleep Cycle
- Waterllama

Glossary

A

agender: A person who does not identify with any gender.

ally: Someone who is supportive of LGBTQ+ individuals and the community, either personally or as an advocate. Allies include heterosexual, cisgender, and LGBTQ+ people who advocate for LGBTQ+ people.

androgynous: An individual with elements of both femininity and masculinity, whether expressed through sex, gender identity, gender expression, or sexual orientation, is known as an androgyne (an-druh-jahyn). (Hermaphroditism is the presence of both male and female reproductive organs in plants and animals. This is a careful distinction. A human is an androgyne. A plant or animal is a hermaphrodite. Calling a person a hermaphrodite is incorrect as well as offensive.)

aromantic/aro: An individual who does not experience romantic attraction.

asexual: One who does not experience sexual attraction. Asexuality is a sexual orientation that does not necessarily include celibacy or sexual abstinence.

assigned gender: The gender that is assigned to an infant at birth, which may or may not align with their sex at birth.

assigned sex: The biological sex that is assigned to an infant at birth based on the child's visible sex organs, including genitalia and other physical characteristics.

B

bigender: Someone who identifies with two distinct genders, such as man/woman or woman/androgyne. Bigender people don't necessarily identify with each gender 50 percent of the time, and unlike gender-fluid people, they don't exist on a spectrum either.

biological sex: Anatomical, physiological, genetic, or physical attributes that determine if a person is male, female, or intersex.

- These attributes include both primary and secondary sex characteristics, including genitalia, gonads, hormone levels, hormone receptors, chromosomes, and genes.
- Often referred to as "sex," "physical sex," "anatomical sex," or specifically as "sex assigned at birth."
- Sex is often confused or interchanged with gender. While sex is biological, gender is social and involves personal identity factors as well.

bisexual: An individual who has the capacity for attraction—sexually, romantically, emotionally—to people of the same or different sex as themself. It is attraction and self-identification that determine orientation. Sometimes referred to as bi or bi+. Identifying as bisexual is not a phase, nor are bisexual people "on their way" to being gay or lesbian. Bisexuality is a sexual orientation (the "B" in LGBTQ+) and not an experimental or transitional stage.

- DO identify people accurately. If they say they are bisexual, bi, or bi+, do not identify them as gay, lesbian, or straight based on who they are in a relationship with.
- DON'T equate bisexuality with promiscuity. It is not only inaccurate; it is harmful.
- DON'T assert that bisexuality is a phase or state of confusion or indecision.
- DO be aware of the bi+ community, which includes, but is not limited to, pansexual, polysexual, omnisexual, fluid, and queer.
- DON'T assume. ASK others how they identify.

C

cisgender: An individual whose gender identity aligns with the sex assigned to them at birth.

closeted: A person who is not open/has not shared their sexual orientation or gender identity.

coming out: For LGBTQ+ people, the process of self-identifying and self-acceptance that continues throughout one's life and the sharing of their orientation and/or identity with others. There are many different stages of the coming out process. Additionally, one may be out to friends only, out publicly, or out to oneself only. It is VITAL to remember that coming out is a deeply personal and transformative experience. Not everyone is in the same place when it comes to being out, and it is of utmost importance to respect where each person is in that process. *The decision of when and if to come out is up to the individual and the individual alone.*

conversion therapy: The disproven and discredited practice of "curing" LGBTQ+ people of their sexual orientation, gender identity, or gender expression "choices" so they adhere to heterosexual and cisgender norms. Conversion therapy has been widely condemned by ALL major medical, psychiatric, and psychological organizations. As of August 2022, twenty-two states and one hundred municipalities have enacted bans on the practice. Not only are these practices harmful and abusive, but there is a growing body of evidence that shows that LGBTQ+ people who have gone through these programs have suffered trauma, depression, and suicidal thoughts and actions at the rate of 2 times their LGBTQ+ peers.

D

deadname: In many cases, a transgender or gender nonconforming person may change their birth name or legal name to a name that aligns better with who they authentically are. When another refers to them by their birth/legal name instead of the name they have requested to be called, it is called deadnaming.

drag queen/king: First and foremost, being a drag queen/king is an art form or creative form of expression, not a gender identity, gender expression, or sexual orientation. A drag queen is a person who performs as a woman for an audience. Likewise, a drag king is a person who performs as a man for an audience. "Performers" and "art form" are the important distinguishing words.

G

gay: The adjective used to describe people who are emotionally, romantically, and/or physically attracted to people of the same sex. People who are gay need not have had any sexual experience; it is the attraction and self-identification that determine orientation. While not exclusively identifying men, it is most often used to describe men.

genderqueer: Individuals who identify as a combination of man and woman, neither man nor woman, or both man and woman; OR someone who rejects commonly held ideas of static gender identities and, occasionally, sexual orientations. It is sometimes used as an umbrella term similar to how the term *queer* is used, but only referring to gender, and thus should only be used when self-identifying or quoting someone who self-identifies as genderqueer.

gender-affirming care: This is a patient-centered and holistic approach to supporting a person on their gender journey. It includes social, psychological, behavioral, and medical interventions that range from therapy to employing the use of pronouns to hormone therapy, etc.

gender dysphoria: The distress caused when a person's assigned sex at birth and assumed gender are not the same as the one with which they identify.

gender expression: The way a person communicates gender to others through external means such as clothing, appearance, or mannerisms.

gender fluid: One who does not identify with a single or a fixed gender. This person may identify on a spectrum or may move along the spectrum, hence *fluid*.

gender identity: One's deeply held core sense of being a woman, man, some of both, or neither. Gender exists on a continuum and can be fluid. One's gender identity does not always correspond to biological sex. Awareness of gender identity is experienced as early as eighteen months old.

gender neutral: Not gendered. Can refer to language (including pronouns and titles), spaces (like bathrooms), or identities (being genderqueer, for example). Pronouns may include they/them/theirs.

gender nonconforming/gender expansive/gender diverse: Terms used to describe one whose gender expression is different from conventional expectations of masculinity and femininity. More current terms include *differently gendered, gender creative, gender variant, genderqueer, nonbinary, agender, gender fluid, gender neutral, bigender, androgynous.* These terms are not synonyms for transgender and should ONLY be used if someone self-identifies as one of the above.

gender socialization: How an individual is taught and influenced to behave based on their gender identity. Parents, teachers, peers, media, and books are some of the many influencers of gender socialization.

gender spectrum: The concept the gender exists beyond a simple male/female binary model and instead exists on a continuum. Some people are more masculine or more feminine, some move fluidly along the spectrum, and some identify off the spectrum entirely.

H

heterosexual: A person who is emotionally, romantically, and/or physically attracted to a person of the opposite sex.

homophobia: Negative feelings or actions towards gay or lesbian people that present as aversion, fear, or hatred and often manifest in the form of violence, discrimination, prejudice, and/or bias.

homosexual: A person who is emotionally, romantically, and/or physically attracted to a person of the same sex.

I

intersectionality: The way the complex and overlapping traits that make up one's identity (i.e., sexual orientation, gender identity, race, ethnicity, ability, socioeconomic status, language, size, religion, etc.) come together and shape their experiences and interactions. Prejudice and discrimination related to these overlapping traits are unique and are different from that faced by people with each individual trait.

intersex: Intersex is the current term used to refer to people who are biologically between the medically expected definitions of male and female. This can be through variations in hormones, chromosomes, internal or external genitalia, or any combination of sex characteristics. Intersex is about biological sex. Fun fact: there are approximately the same number of people born intersex as are born with red hair!

L

lesbian: A woman who is emotionally, romantically, and/or physically attracted to other women. It is attraction, not sexual experience, that determines orientation.

LGBTQIA+: An acronym that collectively refers to individuals who are lesbian, gay, bisexual, transgender, queer, intersex, and/or asexual. The "+" represents those who are part of the community but for whom LGBTQIA does not accurately capture or reflect their identity.

M

microaggression: A commonly encountered comment or behavior toward a marginalized group that is hurtful, insulting, or demeaning. The comment may or may not be intentionally insulting.

misgender: To refer to someone, especially a transgender or gender-expansive person, using a word that does not correctly reflect the gender with which they identify, such as a pronoun or form of address.

N

nonbinary: Refers to individuals who identify as neither man nor woman, both man and woman, or a combination of man and woman. It is an identity term which some use exclusively, while others may use it interchangeably with terms like genderqueer, gender creative, gender nonconforming, gender diverse, or gender expansive.

O

out: Generally describes people who openly self-identify as LGBTQIA+ in their private, public, and/or professional lives.

outing: The accidental or deliberate sharing of another person's sexual orientation, gender identity, or gender expression without their explicit consent. Outing is considered disrespectful and a potentially dangerous act for LGBTQIA+ individuals.

P

pansexual: An individual whose emotional, romantic, and/or physical attraction is to people inclusive of all genders and biological sexes. It is sometimes explained as one's soul's attraction to another's soul. It is this attraction and self-identification that determines the orientation.

Q

queer: A term used by some people to describe themselves and/or their community. It can be inclusive of the entire community and an appropriate term to describe more fluid identities. Because it used to be a negative term for people who are gay, "queer" is still sometimes disliked within the LGBTQIA+ community. This word should only be used when self-identifying or quoting someone who self-identifies as queer.

queerphobia: The fear, bias, and judgment of LGBTQIA+ people. It can also be the actions of bullying, discrimination, lack of acceptance, etc. Whereas homophobia is fear, bias, and/or judgment of gay and/ or lesbian people, queerphobia encompasses all sexual orientation and gender identity phobias, including biphobia, transphobia, and homophobia.

questioning: Those who are in a process of discovery and exploration about their sexual orientation, gender identity, gender expression, or a combination thereof.

S

sexual orientation: Emotional, romantic, or sexual feelings toward other people. It is the attraction that helps determine orientation, not sexual behavior.

T

transgender: A term describing a person's gender identity that does not necessarily match their assigned sex at birth. Transgender people may or may not decide to alter their bodies hormonally and/or surgically to match their gender identity. This word is also used as an umbrella term to describe groups of people who transcend conventional expectations of gender identity or expression, such as people who identify as genderqueer, gender variant, gender diverse, and androgynous. Avoid *transgenders, a transgender,* and *transgendered.* Use *transgender people/ person.*

transition: The process—social, legal, and/or medical—one goes through to discover and/or affirm one's gender identity. This may include taking hormones or hormone blockers, having surgeries, and/ or changing names, pronouns, identification documents, etc. The process for medical transition requires many steps and must be monitored by a doctor-led support team. Recommendations and laws for minimum ages are complex and changing, but some treatments are available for minors. Many individuals choose not to or are unable to transition for a wide range of reasons, both within and beyond their control. The validity of an individual's gender identity does not depend on any social, legal, and/or medical transition; the self-identification itself is what validates the gender identity.

transphobia: Negative feelings or actions towards transgender people that present as aversion, fear, or hatred and often manifest in the form of violence, discrimination, prejudice, and/or bias.

two-spirit: This term is specific to Indigenous people and culture. While not all Indigenous people who are LGBTQIA+ are two-spirit, it is an umbrella term that bridges Indigenous and Western understandings of gender and sexuality.

ACKNOWLEDGMENTS

To Steve: Thank you for your never-ending support, feedback, patience, friendship, and beautiful love. I cherish you and our extraordinary life together.

To Connor: Thank you for allowing me to share your story—and our story—with the world. Your vulnerability has touched so many lives. I treasure our deep connection and the candor of our relationship. Your sharp wit, self-awareness, creative genius, and earned perspective are gifts to all who know you.

To Isabelle: Thank you for sharing your world with me, both internal and external. I am in awe of your resilience and character, and I love the ease and honesty of our relationship.

To Grace: Thank you for being so fabulously you; for not being afraid to challenge stereotypes, for going after your dreams, and for sharing your heart with me. Your wisdom and pragmatism have steadied me more than once!

To Rowan: Thank you for making me laugh and for being so good at shifting the energy of our house in the best way! You have the kindest heart and I love every minute I get to spend with you.

To my sweet family of five: It is an honor and a gift to be married to my best friend and be the mom of the four most exquisite human beings. I am grateful for each of you every day.

To Teagan and Mackenzie: Teagan, I will forever be grateful for your sweet, calming energy and your loyal presence in my office. You were the true teacher of unconditional love. I miss you already. Mackenzie, thank you for your comic relief and overjoyed greetings. You are a gift and beautiful reminder for staying present.

To the members of both of our families who have loved and supported us unconditionally—thank you, truly.

To the best girlfriends a girl could ever ask for, Michelle, Kristen, Maria, and Eden: Thank you for your unwavering support of my family and me—for scraping me off of the floor, listening to my anguish during the darkest days, making me eat and laugh and exit the safety of my house. I love you all!

To Maureen: Thank you for holding space for me, for showing me compassion and a path forward when things were so hard, and for guiding me on this seven-plus-year journey of healing and evolution.

To Kate Versage: Thank you for meeting Steve and me where we were, for holding our family with such tenderness and compassion, and for teaching us so much! I feel honored to call you a friend.

To Cesar Hawas: Thank you for being the perfect person for Connor at the perfect time. Your love and guidance saved my baby in so many ways; I will forever be grateful for that.

To Daniel Fishburne and all of the professionals we have encountered along the way: Thank you. Each of you had a part in our education and walked with us through pain and growth. Some of you were life-saving, all of you, life-enhancing.

To all of my podcast listeners and clients: Thank you for listening! It is an honor to have the opportunity to connect with you and share my world with you.

To everyone who supported us on this journey and showed us love and kindness every step of the way: Thank you. You know who you are, and we are so very grateful.

To Lisa Sugarman: You are a kindred spirit, and I am so grateful for our connection. Thank you for introducing me to all the lovely people at Familius.

To Familius Publishing: Ashley, Brooke, Michele, and Christopher, thank you for your belief in me and my book.

To Coldplay, Taylor Swift, and Jamie Bower: your music helped me every day of this book-writing journey in all the ways I needed it to, whether it was keeping me in the zone or helping me just let it all go.

NOTES

PILLAR ONE

1. Brené Brown, *The Gifts of Imperfection: 10th Anniversary Edition*, (Center City: Hazeldon Publishing, 2022), 6.

CHAPTER TWO

1. Emily Cronkleton, "10 Breathing Exercises to Try: For Stress, Training, and Lung Capacity," *Healthline*, last modified March 24, 2023, https://www.healthline.com/health/breathing-exercise#pursed-lip-breathing.

CHAPTER THREE

1. Gary Gilles, "7 tips for Effective Communication with Your School-aged Child," MentalHelp.net, May 22, 2014, https://www.mentalhelp.net/blogs/7-tips-for-effective-communication-with-your-school-aged-child/.

CHAPTER FOUR

1. Kira M. Newman, "Five Science-Backed Strategies to Build Resilience," *Greater Good Magazine*, November 9, 2016, https://greatergood.berkeley.edu/article/item/five_science_backed_strategies_to_build_resilience.

PILLAR TWO

1. "It's Intersex Awareness Day—Here Are 5 Myths We Need to Shatter," Amnesty.org, 26 October 2018, https://www.amnesty.org/en/latest/news/2018/10/its-intersex-awareness-day-here-are-5-myths-we-need-to-shatter/#:~:text=Myth%202%3A%20Being%20intersex%20is,intersex%20people%20are%20massively%20underrepresented.

CHAPTER FIVE

1. Suzanne Degges-White, Barbara Rice, and Jane E. Myers, "Revisiting Cass' theory of sexual identity formation: A study of lesbian development," *Journal of Mental Health Counseling* 22, no. 4 (2000): 318-333. https://libres.uncg.edu/ir/uncg/f/j_myers_revisiting_2000.pdf.

2. Vivienne Cass PhD, *Quick Guide to the Cass Theory of Lesbian and Gay Identity Formation*, (Bentley, AUS: Brightfire Press, 2015), 53.

3. Ibid., 55.

4. Ibid., 57.

5. Ibid.

6. Ibid., 59.

7. Ibid., 61.

8. Ibid., 63.

CHAPTER SIX

1. "The Journey for Parents," Strong Family Alliance, accessed July 25, 2023, https://www.strongfamilyalliance.org/parent-guides/parent-guide-gay/the-journey-for-parents/.

CHAPTER SEVEN

1. 1. "Boundaries: What are they and how to create them," Wellness Center University of Illinois Chicago, 25 February 2022, https://wellnesscenter.uic.edu/news-stories/boundaries-what-are-they-and-how-to-create-them/. Accessed 24 February 2023.

CHAPTER NINE

1. Heather Hester, "You Said It: Local Mom Opens Up About Son's Battle With Depression, Shares Message of Hope," *Better*, October 23, 2018, https://better.net/chicago/life/family/local-mom-opens-up-about-sons-battle-with-depression-lgbtq-awareness/.

2. "The State of Mental Health in America," Mental Health America, accessed July 18, 2023, https://mhanational.org/issues/state-mental-health-america.

3. "2023 U.S. National Survey on the Mental Health of LGBTQ Young People," The Trevor Project, accessed June 26, 2023, https://www.thetrevorproject.org/survey-2023/.

4. "Youth Mental Health: Trends and Outlook," National Institute for Health Care Management, last modified February 22, 2021, https://nihcm.org/publications/youth-mental-health-trends-and-outlook.

5. Ilan H. Meyer et al., "Suicidal Behavior and Coming Out Milestones in Three Cohorts of Sexual Minority Adults," *LGBT Health* (July 2021): 340-348, http://doi.org/10.1089/lgbt.2020.0466.

6. "Self-Harm," Psychology Today, accessed July 18, 2023, https://www.psychologytoday.com/us/basics/self-harm.

7. Lauren M. O'Reilly et al., "Sexual Orientation and Adolescent Suicide Attempt and Self-harm: a Co-twin Control Study," *The Journal for Child Phscology and Psychiatry* 62, no 7 (September 14, 2020):834-841, https://acamh.onlinelibrary.wiley.com/doi/abs/10.1111/jcpp.13325.

8. Bonnie Harmer et al., *Suicidal Ideation* (Treasure Island (FL): StatPearls Publishing, 2023), https://pubmed.ncbi.nlm.nih.gov/33351435/.

9. Stephanie Pappas, "More Than 20% of Teens Have Seriously Considered Suicide. Psychologists and Communities Can help Tackle the Problem," *Monitor on Psychology* 54, no. 5 (July/August 2023):54, https://www.apa.org/monitor/2023/07/psychologists-preventing-teen-suicide.

10. E. David Klonsky, Titiana Dizon-Luinenburg, and Alexis M. May, "The Critical Distinction Between Suicidal Ideation and Suicide Attempts," *World Psychiatry* 20, no.3 (October 2021):439-441, doi:10.1002/wps.20909.

11. "Suicide," World Health Organization, 28 August 28, 2023, Accessed November 2, 2023, https://www.who.int/health-topics/suicide#tab=tab_1

12. "Facts About LGBTQ Suicide," The Trevor Project, December 15, 2021, accessed October 30, 2023, https://www.thetrevorproject.org/resources/article/facts-about-lgbtq-youth-suicide/.

13. Ibid.

14. Dr, Craig Bryan et al., Effect of crisis response planning vs. contracts for safety on suicide risk in U.S. Army Soldiers: A randomized clinical trial, *Journal of Affective Disorders* 212 (2017): 64-72, https://doi.org/10.1016/j.jad.2017.01.028.

15. AnneMoss Rogers, "How Can You Create a Mental Health Coping Card?" Mental Health Awareness Education, October 12, 2023, https://mentalhealthawarenesseducation.com/how-can-you-create-a-mental-health-coping-card/.

CHAPTER TEN

1. "Part 1: The Connection Between Substance Use Disorders and Mental Illness," National Institute on Drug Abuse, September 27, 2022, https://nida.nih.gov/publications/research-reports/common-comorbidities-substance-use-disorders/part-1-connection-between-substance-use-disorders-mental-illness.

2. "United States, High School Youth Risk Behavior Survey, 2021," Centers for Disease Control and Prevention, Accessed August 2, 2023, https://nccd.cdc.gov/Youthonline/

3. "Using the Icelandic Model to Prevent Teenage Substance Use," ASTHO, October 9, 2019, https://www.astho.org/communications/blog/using-icelandic-model-to-prevent-teenage-substance-use/.

4. "SAMHSA Releases New Data on Lesbian, Gay and Bisexual Behavioral Health," Substance Abuse and Mental Health Services Administration, June 13, 2023, https://www.samhsa.gov/newsroom/press-announcements/20230613/samhsa-releases-new-data-lesbian-gay-bisexual-behavioral-health.

5. Krissy Potatek, "4 Reasons It's Important for Parents to Set Healthy Boundaries with Kids," Mindbodygreen, November 30, 2020, https://www.mindbodygreen.com/articles/healthy-boundaries-in-parenting.

CHAPTER ELEVEN

1. Kristen Neff, PhD and Christopher Germer, PhD, *The Mindful Self-Compassion Workbook: A Proven Way to Accept Yourself, Build Inner Strength, and Thrive* (New York: Guilford Press, 2018), 39.

2. Jo Nash, "How to Set Healthy Boundaries & Build Positive Relationships," *Positive Psychology*, January 5, 2018, https://positivepsychology.com/great-self-care-setting-healthy-boundaries/.

3. Kirsten Waters, *Struggle Guru: The Biographical Struggles that are Influencing Our Biology* (Pennsauken Township: BookBaby, 2020), 23-28.

4. Kirsten Waters, *Struggle Guru: The Biographical Struggles that are Influencing Our Biology* (Pennsauken Township: BookBaby, 2020), 25.

PILLAR THREE

1. *Oxford Languages Online*, s.v. "empower," accessed July 24, 2023, https://www.google.com/search?q=dictionary+definition+of+empower.

CHAPTER TWELVE

1. *Cambridge Dictionary Online*, s.v. "advocate," accessed July 26, 2023, https://dictionary.cambridge.org/dictionary/learner-english/advocate.

2. *Cambridge dictionary Online*, s.v. "advocate," accessed August 2, 2023, https://dictionary.cambridge.org/us/dictionary/english/advocate.

CHAPTER FOURTEEN

1. "5 Ways to Develop Your Intuition," Deepak Chopra, July 6, 2016, https://www.deepakchopra.com/articles/5-ways-to-develop-your-intuition/.

CHAPTER FIFTEEN

1. William J. Hall, Hayden C. Dawes, and Nina Plocek, "Sexual Orientation Identity Development Milestones Among Lesbian, Gay, Bisexual, and Queer People: A Systematic Review and Meta-Analysis," *Frontiers in Psychology* 12, (October 21, 2021):2, doi:10.3389/fpsyg.2021.753954.

2. Ibid, 2-3.

3. Hester, Heather. *Just Breathe: Parenting Your LGBTQ Teen* podcast, Ep. 16 "When It Feels Scary." https://player.captivate.fm/episode/46326110-778b-4ac9-8571-9a697ed4c61f

4. "Meditation," Chrysalis Mama, accessed October 30, 2023, https://chrysalismama.com/meditation?lightbox=dataItem-jn3wdr9z1.

CHAPTER SIXTEEN

1. Deborah Khoshaba, "A Seven-Step Prescription for Self-Love," *Psychology Today*, March 27, 2012, https://www.psychologytoday.com/us/blog/get-hardy/201203/seven-step-prescription-self-love.

CHAPTER SEVENTEEN

1. Gary Chapman, *The 5 Love Languages of Teenagers: The Secret to Loving Teens Effectively* (New York: Northfield Publishing, 2016), 66.

2. Shauna Tominey, "Five Ways to Talk with Your Kids So They Feel Loved," *Greater Good Magazine*, March 18, 2019, https://greatergood.berkeley.edu/article/item/ five_ways_to_talk_with_your_kids_so_they_feel_loved.

3. Eden Pontz, "The Power of Love in Protecting Children," Center for Parent and Teen Communication, Sep 14, 2022, https://parentandteen.com/power-of-love-in-raising-children/.

CHAPTER EIGHTEEN

1. Elizabeth Earnshaw, "Unconditional Love: How to Give It & Know If It's Healthy," Mindbodygreen, April 14, 2023, https://www.mindbodygreen.com/articles/ understanding-unconditional-love.

About the Author

Heather Hester is the founder of Chrysalis Mama, which provides support and education to parents and allies of LGBTQIA adolescents, teenagers, and young adults. She is also the creator and host of the podcast *Just Breathe: Parenting Your LGBTQ Teen.* As an advocate and coach for parents and allies, she believes the coming out process is equal parts beautiful and messy. She works with her clients to let go of fear and feelings of isolation so that they can reconnect with themselves and their children in a meaningful, grounded way. Heather also works within organizations via workshops and specialized programming to bring education and empowerment with a human touch. She is married to her best friend, is the mother of four extraordinary kids (two of whom are LGBTQIA) and one sassy mini bernedoodle, and is a student of life who believes in being authentic and embracing the messiness.

About Familius

VISIT OUR WEBSITE: WWW.FAMILIUS.COM

Familius is a global trade publishing company that publishes books and other content to help families be happy. We believe that happy families are key to a better society and the foundation of a happy life. The greatest work anyone will ever do will be within the walls of his or her own home. And we don't mean vacuuming! We recognize that every family looks different and passionately believe in helping all families find greater joy, whatever their situation. To that end, we publish books for children and adults that invite families to live the Familius Ten Habits of Happy Families: *love together, play together, learn together, work together, talk together, heal together, read together, eat together, give together,* and *laugh together.* Further, Familius does not discriminate on the basis of race, color, religion, gender, age, nationality, disability, caste, or sexual orientation in any of its activities or operations. Founded in 2012, Familius is located in Sanger, California.

JOIN OUR FAMILY

There are lots of ways to connect with us! Subscribe to our podcast, *Helping Families Be Happy,* and join our newsletters at www.familius.com to receive uplifting daily inspiration, essays from our Pater Familius, a free ebook every month, and the first word on special discounts and Familius news.

CONNECT

Facebook: www.facebook.com/familiusbooks
Twitter: @FamiliusBooks
Pinterest: www.pinterest.com/familiusbooks
Instagram: @FamiliusBooks
TikTok: @FamiliusBooks

The most important work you ever do
will be within the walls of your own home.